Tennessee Williams on the Soviet Stage

Irene Shaland

UNIVERSITY
PRESS OF
AMERICA

LANHAM • NEW YORK • LONDON

Copyright © 1987 by

University Press of America,® Inc.

4720 Boston Way
Lanham, MD 20706

3 Henrietta Street
London WC2E 8LU England

All rights reserved

Printed in the United States of America

British Cataloging in Publication Information Available

Library of Congress Cataloging-in-Publication Data

Shaland, Irene, 1955-
 Tennessee Williams on the Soviet stage.

 Bibliography: p.
 1. Williams, Tennessee, 1911-   —Stage hstory—
Soviet Union. 2. Theater—Soviet Union—History—20th
century. I. Title.
PS3545.I5365Z834   1987   812'.54   86-32506
ISBN 0-8191-6109-8 (alk. paper)

All University Press of America books are produced on acid-free
paper which exceeds the minimum standards set by the National
Historical Publication and Records Commission.

To my mother whose
love and talent enabled
me to start writing

ACKNOWLEDGMENTS

This work could not have been written without the stimulation, encouragement, and help I have received from my Soviet friends.

To Professor Robert Ornstein (Case Western Reserve University, English Department) I owe an enormous debt of thanks since it was his teaching that inspired me to start this project in the first place, just as it was his continued interest and advice that enabled me to see it through to the end.

I also wish to express my endless gratitude to my friend Doctor Harold Tatar. He contributed to this work not only by helping to edit the manuscript but also by sharing with me, in many conversations, his deep knowledge in a wide range of material relevant to the phenomenon of Tennessee Williams in the Soviet theatre.

I am especially indebted to my dear friend Meg Cole for her enthusiasm about this book that provided me with strength when I needed it most and for her wise and sensitive editing.

Finally, my husband, Alex, has helped me immeasurably by continuing to believe both in the worth of this project and in my ability to bring it to a successful conclusion.

Irene Shaland

Cleveland, Ohio, December, 1985

TABLE OF CONTENTS

Chapter   Page

Acknowledgments v

I   Instead of an Introduction 1

II   The Beginning: <u>A</u> <u>Streetcar</u> <u>Named</u> <u>Desire</u> on the Moscow Stage 11

III The Endless Journey: Comprehending Williams <u>The</u> <u>Glass</u> <u>Menagerie</u> on the Soviet Stage 23

IV   Orpheus Castrated: <u>Orpheus</u> <u>Descending</u> and <u>Sweet</u> <u>Bird</u> <u>of</u> <u>Youth</u> on the Moscow Stages 41

V   Struggle for Property or World Before the Flood: <u>Kingdom</u> <u>of</u> <u>Earth</u> in Moscow and Leningrad 67

Epilogue 89

"It is a belief still pre-eminently honored that a primary function of art and thought is to liberate the individual from the tyranny of his culture in the environmental sense and to permit him to stand beyond it in anatomy of perception and judgement."

Lionel Trilling.

CHAPTER I

INSTEAD OF AN INTRODUCTION

The Soviet theatre has survived the assassination of its leaders, the dark age of personality cult, the furious fight against cosmopolitanism, and the time when the only possible subject of drama could be the so-called "struggle of the good against the best." However, in spite of the iron ideological control, the Soviet theatre remains a most interesting phenomenon. Unfortunately, almost nothing concerning contemporary Soviet theatre is available in the English language. In particular, for the last ten years, nothing has been written in English about American drama on the Soviet stage.[1] This subject, however, may be of interest for many groups: to those who study American-Russian cultural interrelationships, for example, or to those who are concerned with the problems inherent in the translation and transposition of drama. It may, in fact, be of interest to anyone who loves and cares about modern theatre.

The principal aim of the present paper is to focus on one particular American dramatist, Tennessee Williams, and to explore the problems involved in staging his works in the Soviet theatre.

Almost forty years ago Lee Simonson wrote in his "Introduction" to Norris Houghton's book, <u>Moscow Rehearsals</u>: "For the artist all roads once led to Rome; yesterday to Paris. Today, for the artist in the theatre, whether actor, director, or designer, the road leads to Moscow and the theatres of the U.S.S.R."[2]

Indeed, the twenties and thirties were the years of experiment and discovery on the Soviet stage; without them one cannot imagine the development of twentieth-century theatre. However, this short bright period marked by artistic creativity was followed by a long, dark night of ideological pressure and the annihilation of any suspected talent and originality.

One of the mysterious and key figures of the modern theatre, Vsevolod Meyerkhold, accused Party officials when he spoke at the All-Union Conference of Stage-directors:

> Not so long ago creative thought was flourishing. Artists made

mistakes but experimented freely. Sometimes they created failures; at other times--wonders. But now, thanks to you, where the best theatres of the world once existed, there we find despondency and mediocrity. Is that what you wanted? If yes, oh! You have achieved a great success: you have destroyed art!3

It was June, 1939. Two days days later, Meyerkhold was arrested and soon died in one of the concentration camps.

The development of modern Russian theatre has been uneven. There were dull, colorless years when the whole meaning of creative labor disappeared and art was converted into ideological propaganda. There was also a time of "thaw,"4 and the partial lifting of the iron curtain between the Soviet Union and the Western world. Little by little, European and American literature and drama began to penetrate the culture that had been closed to any "alien" influence since the thirties.

At the end of the forties, during the period of furious attacks against "cosmopolitanism," Tennessee Williams was mentioned in the Soviet press for the first time. <u>Literaturnaya Gazeta</u> (Literary Weekly Newspaper) reported on the staging of a play "with the wild name <u>A Streetcar Named Desire</u> written by a certain Williams."5 The moral degradation and spiritual decay in capitalistic society "run into absurdity,"5 commented the newspaper. However, in 1956, the journal <u>Inostrannaya Literatura</u> (Foreign Literature) was resurrected (it had been called <u>International Literature</u> and was closed in 1936); and the works of "certain" authors began to be translated: among others, Ernest Hemingway, James Aldridge, John Osborne.

The latter, so respected for his "anger" toward capitalistic reality, brought an unexpected disappointment. Having been invited to the Moscow International Youth Festival in 1957, he left before the festivities had concluded. It was one of the first times when the Soviet capital was opened to foreign tourists and delegations. The English playwright, irritated by the atmosphere of ostentation, magnificence and feigned prosperity, was said to comment: "To some, Moscow covered by snow and bathed in sunshine, with her troubadours hawking peace slogans, might have seemed a wedding cake, but to me it seemed a wild provincial nightmare." He also was said to refer to the Soviet writers as a "terrible conformist mob." The aggrieved Literaturnaya Gazeta wrote: "How the neurasthenic has degenerated."6

Nevertheless, the infiltration of Western culture into Soviet society was already irreversible. The post-Stalin iron curtain was definitely lifting.

The theatres of Moscow were beginning to open their doors to Western companies. The first to come, in 1954, was La Comedie Francaise with Moliere and Corneille. French classical drama was very well known and popular in the Soviet Union. Stanislavsky's Figaro's Wedding had become a classic of the Russian modern theatre. The wonderful Tartuffe with Toporkov in the title role was still one of the best performances on the MXAT (Moscow Artistic Academic Theatre) stage. But the acting style of the French proved to be entirely different from traditional Russian theatrical realism. It possessed lightness, elegance, and irony combined with a touch of the grotesque to form an absolutely different plasticity, a different scenic existence. For the whole generation of actors and spectators it was a discovery.

Then, in 1957, came the TNP theatre from Paris with Musset, Hugo, and Balzac. That same year, the Berliner Ensemble introduced Brecht to the Moscow public with his brilliant Mother Courage starring Helene Weigel. In the early sixties, the following foreign companies arrived in close succession: from Italy, Franco Zeffirelli's group with Anna Magnani and the Piccolo Teatro di Milano; from Athens, the Theatre of Greek Tragedy ; from England, the Royal, Old Vic, Stratford-upon-Avon theatres; and from France, the Vieux Colombier. The latter, when it came in 1960, introduced Anouilh's The Lark.

Theatrical Moscow became excited. Against the generally dull backround, striking individual productions began to stand out. In the Mayakovsky Theatre, the remarkable Soviet stage-director Okhlopkov produced Brecht's The Threepenny Opera and The Caucasian Chalk Circle. The Sovremennik theatre company (Contemporary) with young Oleg Efremov as director (now he is an obedient Artistic Director in the MXAT) impudently announced itself as a theatre-innovator. For the first time after many years, American drama appeared on the stage.[7] Sovremennik turned to young Edward Albee. It was not Albee-"absurdist" with his Zoo Story but Albee of The Death of Bessie Smith and the The Ballad of the Sad Cafe.

Then there was another splash: in 1964 a new theatre was born--Theatre on Taganka, created by the energy and will of Yuri Liubimov, a stage-director of genius. Twenty years later this striking, world-famous theatre would be destroyed, his productions banned, when Liubimov, sick and tired of the endless struggle with the authorities over each play, would leave for England. But in 1964, there was no suggestion of the trouble that lay ahead.

In the foyer of his theatre, Liubimov placed four portraits: Stanislavsky, Meyerkhold, Vakhtangov, and Brecht. He wanted his company to develop a new theatrical art: a wonderful fusion of folk farce, scenic abstraction, music, and classical Russian psychological theatre. Brecht's The Good Woman of Setzuan opened Theatre on Taganka. This Brecht was different from the realistic productions of Okhlopkov. An element of real theatricality was revived--alienation, irony, festivity. Meyerkhold and Vakhtangov seemed to be alive again. How did it happen? With the help of Brecht? By the power of time? Moscovites, greedy for theatrical news, were taking by storm the box offices of those theatres where one could inhale at least a breath of fresh air.

The first performance of Tennessee Williams appeared in this atmosphere. In 1960, the magazine Inostrannaya Literatura published a translation of Orpheus Descending. In 1961, this play was staged in the Mossoviet Theatre by the director Anisimova-Vulf. V. Vulf (he is the translator and drama critic who holds the "monopoly" on the "Soviet" Williams) wrote: "The actual acquaintance with Williams's drama in our country began as far back as in 1961 when the Mossoviet Theatre staged his Orpheus."[8] However, Anisimova-Vulf's performance was marked by the extreme simplification of the play's philosophical problems. Williams's drama became a condemnation of the American South where Val and Carol appeared as rebels.

This production could not acquaint the Soviet public with the real Tennessee Williams. Probably the first true meeting of the American playwright and a Soviet audience occurred in 1967, twenty years after

Williams had become famous all over the world. It was the publication of an anthology of ten of Williams's plays, well-translated by Yakov Bereznitsky, a movie and drama critic. (<u>The Glass Menagerie and Nine Other Plays</u>, Moscow: Iskusstvo, 1967) The book at once became a bibliographical rarity.

Eight years after the Mossoviet <u>Orpheus</u>, the Ermolova Theatre made another attempt at Williams's drama by staging <u>The Glass Menagerie</u>. This production also was not a success. But two years later, in 1971, <u>A Streetcar Named Desire</u> was staged in the Mayakovsky Theatre (in Moscow) and became the subject of a bitter controversy. It was a real theatrical and intellectual event. This production actually opened a road to the Soviet stage for Williams, and it marked the beginning of his true existence as an integral part of Russian spiritual life. During the seventies and the first half of the eighties, Tennessee Williams became a favorite Western playwright, and also one of the most frequently staged authors in the Soviet theatre.

The phenomenon of this popularity will be explored in the present paper. This work will deal primarily with some major productions of Tennessee Williams in the capital and in provincial theatres. These are productions that reflect characteristic peculiarities of translating American drama not only into the Russian language but also "into" the Russian stage with its strong performing traditions.

In the current repertoire of the Soviet theatre there are almost two hundred works by modern foreign authors. But when we turn from the numbers to every-day practice, we see that there is often one author whom--for some reason incomprehensible to most outside observers--all theatres want to stage simultaneously. This became the case with Williams.

One might say that this phenomenon of Williams's seemingly sudden popularity on the Soviet stage happened by chance. It may also be attributed to the energy of the influential Williams's Soviet translator, V. Vulf. (Not only is he the translator of the majority of staged Williams's plays, as I suggested earlier, but he is also the author of the majority of published articles on Williams). Then too there has been the desire of various famous actors to play important Williams's roles. In real life, especially in the theatre, we cannot leave subjective factors out of consideration. But on the other hand, neither should they be overrated.

For many reasons, the appearance of Williams on the Soviet stage in the fifties--the time of his triumph in many other parts of the world--was impossible. But in the seventies, the Russian theatrical discovery of Williams happened almost simultaneously with a revival of interest in this playwright in his native country. After the "Stoned Age" of the sixties (his own expression), the time of his deepest depression, Williams was again received as a literary maestro. He also achieved the status of a "living classic" in American literature, and his old plays took on a new life. Perhaps people started to find Williams's values more compelling.

Yet there is a tendency for the Soviet critics to consider Williams as a prophet who is misunderstood in his native land. "He creates plays," writes Vulf, "filled with pain and discord--major signs of the American spiritual situation."[9] Another drama critic, V. Nedelin, wrote in his article published in the first book of Williams's plays:

> While he seems to advocate the ˜shameless romanticism˜of human existence, in reality Williams seeks to explore those bourgeois social relationships that doom a man to psychological isolation. Hence the guilt, violence and black despair that fill his dramas.[10]

Thus Soviet drama critics reduce Williams's tragic and poetic art to a simple denunciation of capitalistic "consumer society" guilty of "destroying spirit, souls, and destinies." "The playwright clearly leads the audience to think of the crisis of bourgeois civilization,"[11] says Vulf. It has become commonplace for critics of Williams to stress the "lack of convergence" between the "official ideology of the U.S.A." (a typical Soviet formulation) and Williams's values. For example, Vulf in another review writes:

> The search for ˜pure˜ emotional experience, the substitution of feeling for thinking, the disregard of discipline ... Here are the historical features of American

culture. Now these same features dominate American ˜mass culture,˜ which is characterized by a cult of force and irrational violence. This culture has its foundation in the ˜mass subconsciousness˜ ruled by covert feelings of terror, helplessness, and a lack of faith in man and his abilities to orient himself in the world. But Williams, on the other hand, believes that the only conceivable dignity of man lies in his ability to choose his own ideals and to live without waiving his rights.12

In other words, could not this artist be appreciated only in Soviet criticism? "To choose his own ideals by himself and live without waiving his rights"--does it not perfectly fit the Soviet system? "Williams's nonconformism," concludes Vulf, "clearly withstands the dogmas and ideas of today's America. Solitude and disappointment, pride and artistic fearlessness--this is the lot of a man who cannot be a prophet in his own country."13

However, Williams as he appears on the Soviet stage, was not so simplisticly interpreted as in the pages of the major publications. The comprehension of his art by the Soviet theatre has been a very complicated and uneven process. It has turned to Williams for more than a powerful attack on American society. For the Russian stage, with its strong psychological and realistic traditions and its innate interest in the life of the human spirit, Williams has been attractive because of his ability to peer into the depths of human nature without abusive curiosity but with understanding and compassion. Also important for the Russian theatre has been Williams's concept of people's eternal need for one another--a need strong enough to overcome arrogance, brutality, and egoism.

Sometimes the American playwright was seen through Chekhov, sometimes through Dostoevsky. Sometimes his characters were acted as in realistic and psychological drama. In the traditional Russian theatre, an actor has, first of all, to master the physical life of his hero. He has to find, as Stanislavsky taught, the chain of his character's physical actions that have made up his life. A scenic image is formed from the actor's ability to live his hero's physical life; to find for him the most characteristic and striking features, and, at the same time, to accumulate the secret treasures of the character's psychology.

In Williams's plastic theatre, however, his characters act in obedience to different laws. Thus when a theatre different in tradition and necessarily reactive to ideological state control, sets out to comprehend the artistic specification of Williams's symbolic dramas, it must result in a long and complicated process. It cannot be completed within the limits of a dozen productions. Perhaps this process can be more easily explained if we leave chronological sequence and start our discussion with a performance that marked Williams's arrival as one of the most popular and frequently performed dramatists on the modern Soviet stage.

NOTES

1 Computer Data Base Search, Freiberger Library, Case Western Reserve University, July 1985.

2 Lee Simonson, "Introduction," in Moscow Rehearsals, by Norris Houghton (New York: Grove, 1966), p. xi.

3 G. Volkov, "Meyerkhold Kakim On Byl," Novoe Russkoe Slovo, 31 Avg. 1984. (G. Volkov, "Meyerkhold-- As He Really Was," The New Russian Word, 31 Aug. 1984).

4 Ilya Erenburg, a famous Soviet writer, so named his novel about the fifties--The Thaw.

5 From the personal report.

6 From the personal report.

7 Perhaps with the exception of Lillian Hellman's Little Foxes staged in 1945 by the Moscow Drama Theatre with Faina Ranevskaya.

8 V. Vulf, "Tennessi Uilyams i Ego Pesa," v Teatralnoy Programme k spektaklyu Tsarstvie Zemnoe. Moskovsky Teatr imeni Mossoveta, 1977. (V. Vulf, "Tennessee Williams and His Play," in the Theatre Program for the production of Kingdom of Earth, Moscow Mossoviet Theatre, 1977).

9 V. Vulf, "Vozvrashchenie Tennessi Uilyamsa," v V. Vulf, Ot Brodveya Nemnogo v Storonu (Moskva: Iskusstvo, 1982), str. 101. (V. Vulf, "The Return of Tennessee Williams," in his A Little Aside of Broadway, p. 101).

10 V. Nedelin, "Doroga Zhizni v Pesakh Tennessi Uilyamsa," v Tennessi Uilyams, Steklyanny Zverinets i Eshche Devyat Pes, perevod Ya. Bereznitskogo (Moskva: Iskusstvo, 1967), str. 352. (V. Nedelin, "The Road of Life in Tennessee Williams's Dramas," in The Glass Menagerie and Nine Other Plays, by Tennessee Williams, trans. Ya. Bereznitsky, p.352).

11 V. Vulf, "Vozvrashchenie Tennessi Uilyamsa," str. 102. (V. Vulf, "The Return of Tennessee Williaws," p. 102).

12 V. Vulf, "Zhivaya Legenda," <u>Teatr</u>, No. 5 (1981), str. 135. (V. Vulf, "The Living Legend," <u>Theatre</u>, p. 135).

13 V. Vulf, "Zhivaya Legenda," str. 136.

CHAPTER II

THE BEGINNING: <u>A STREETCAR NAMED DESIRE</u> ON THE MOSCOW STAGE

In 1971 nobody could recall the article from <u>Literaturnaya Gazeta</u> about the absurdity of Western culture in which such a "wild" play as <u>A Streetcar Named Desire</u> was possible. That year A. Goncharov, the stage-director of the Mayakovsky Theatre, produced <u>Streetcar</u>, at once attracting the attention of critics and audience. The staging of an American play was in itself no longer sensational. In fact, in 1971 two volumes of Eugene O'Neill's dramas, and, in addition, plays of Osborne and Pinter were translated and published. Durrenmatt's ironic <u>The Visit of the Old Lady</u> was a favorite of spectators in Moscow. Anouilh's <u>Thieves' Carnival</u> and <u>Le Rendezvous de Senlis</u> were staged in the Ermolova and Gogol theatres; another Williams's play, <u>The Glass Menagerie</u>, was in the repertoire of the Ermolova. Obviously Western drama had already won itself a firm position on the Moscow stage. What was so different about Goncharov's <u>Streetcar</u> that distinguished this production from many others?

Goncharov saw the main theme of the play as the downfall and ruin of fragile beauty and its incompatibility with the vulgar and cruel world. Of course, this conception is just one of the possible interpretations of the great play. After more than a decade of comprehending Williams's dramas by the Soviet stage, some might have considered Goncharov's theatrical way of thinking as too traditional, even banal. But in Moscow, in 1971, at a time of gross-sociological approach to art, a performance stressing spiritual rather than social conflict was not only a theatrical but an intellectual event.

Goncharov's conception was not easy to realize. The theatre's set designer, Yuri Bogoyavlensky, created a very simple setting. There was no extra detail on the stage; unfortunately there was also little evocation of the trembling world of Williams's drama. Williams gives stage directions which are suggestive but not explicit, such as: "A sky of peculiarly tender blue, almost a turquoise, which invests the scene with a kind of lyricism and gracefully attenuates the atmosphere of decay."[14] The playwright uses the symbolism of nature to segregate the incorruptible, ideal world of man's dreams where "the purity and beauty of sensual life" can exist, from man's jungle world, the "kingdom of earth." The designer outlined the French Quarter on the Mayakovsky stage, but he failed to suggest either the symbolism of nature or the sombre atmosphere of the trap for the white moth, Blanche. Bogoyavlensky seemed to be concerned with paying a tribute to ascetic constructivism of the thirties rather than with trying to understand Williams.

When Goncharov staged Cat on a Hot Tin Roof in 1982, the artist Mark Kitaev made a round pavilion with transparent walls. Different shades and texture of white were used to express the wealth and refinement of Big Daddy's house. The setting looked more like Oscar Wilde than like Williams's South. Williams's theatrical poetics requires something more than repudiation of traditional realistic design; unfortunately, this is not always understood by set designers.

With Goncharov's production of Streetcar there were problems in performance as well as in set design. The success of this play always depends on the actress in the role of Blanche. Goncharov gave it to Svetlana Nemolyaeva. A very gifted actress, one of the leaders in the Mayakovsky theatre, she tried to give her Blanche everything she had. It was not her fault that her artistic nature was not as high-strung as that of Blanche Du Bois. Nemolyaeva chose a distinctive physical manner for her heroine: an affected plasticity with broken movements and intonations. Her Blanche was very close to classical Russian heroines from realistic and psychological literature: an image of female purity on a spiritual quest for love and compassion, with a life doomed by the hostile world. This Blanche came to her sister's house seeking refuge but she had to pay for being beautiful in an ugly world and for craving for love where there was only banality and cruelty. The deep of the sea that she dreams of in the last scene, or the abyss of the madhouse she is taken to is the only reward: a Blanche almost sister to Katerina in Ostrovsky's Thunderstorm! Williams's heroine was interpreted and acted within the traditional limits of the Russian classical theatre.

Williams's poetics is different: his saints and martyrs are composed of the same flesh and blood as the other inhabitants of the hell that surrounds them. He wrote his Blanche as a masterpiece of contradiction.

Her quest is for poetry and beauty: magic and poetry are her retreat from reality. Nemolyaeva did try to express this quest but the spirituality of her Blanche was externally rather than internally created. However, Williams intended the audience to doubt the refinement of Blanche's imagination and to distrust her poetic lies. Sometimes she uses tasteless similes or makes vulgar remarks; she can be rude and rough. Very often her words are proper and poetic, but her deeds are impulsive and reckless. After all, it is Blanche herself who intrudes into the world of Stanley. Williams never creates heroes and villains, characters who are moral absolutes.

This ambiguity was not understood by the director. What Goncharov wanted to emphasize was the sombre fate of spiritual refinement and beauty with a mental institution as the reward for inner freedom. Blanche's monologue, "maybe we are long way from being made in God's image,"[15] her words about art and poetry that had to be held as a "flag in our march through darkness,"[15] were taken by the company as the major clues to the play. Nemolyaeva spoke this monologue directly to the audience creating an effect of alienation from the role she had been developing, a moment that seemed to belong more to Brecht than to Williams. On the Moscow stage, Blanche was transformed into an instinctive rebel at war with the brutal world of Stanley.

However, not everyone agreed with this interpretation. Drama critic Yuri Zubkov in his angry article, "Even in Defiance of the Play" published in the newspaper Sovetskaya Kultura (Soviet Culture) upbraided the theatre for interpreting Blanche as a "ray of light in the darkness of Stanley's world."[16] (The famous Russian critic Dobrolyubov, over one hundred years earlier, had used the description "the ray of light in the kingdom of darkness" in reference to Ostrovsky's heroine, Katerina, and it had since become a common formula). Zubkov himself believed that the company, in its presentation of Blanche, followed Williams, but he was not convinced that a heroine like her was worth performing on the Soviet stage. From the critic's point of view, Blanche's spirituality, so dear to Goncharov, was "nothing but the veil that covers lewdness."[17] Zubkov wanted, "even in defiance of the play," to dethrone Blanche. His evaluation was merciless. Blanche Du Bois was compared to Sonechka Marmeladova from Dostoevsky's Crime and Punishment; to Nastya from Gorky's The Lower Depth; to women from

Kuprin's The Pit. He wrote: "But if for the Russian classic heroines their way of life was a great tragedy ordained by the prevailing social conditions, Blanche's whole misfortune was a lack of job and money. Her way of life was her chosen element, her poetry."[17] This comparison of Williams's heroine to Russian classical characters was of course arbitrary and tactless, but there was something in Nemolyaeva's portrayal of Blanche that could suggest those allusions.

On the Mayakovsky stage, Blanche's image appeared too simplified. In obedience to Goncharov's directions, Nemolyaeva achieved high emotional tension, but did not portray the depth of the role. The theme of the heroine's guilt regarding her husband's death was completely missing. It was not clear whether the company misunderstood this aspect of the drama along with the ambiguous and painful attitude of Williams toward his Blanche, or whether Blanche's complexity just did not fit into Goncharov's scheme. In any case, in this production the audience was not given the Blanche who had abruptly blurted out the words of contempt that drove her first and only love to suicide. Like Orestes, Williams's heroine had made a guilty choice, a choice which involved her in the sufferings of others. Nemolyaeva did not portray this tragic experience of her heroine, this wound, this mental block which Blanche was not able to overcome. Possibly the limitations of the psychological theatre prevented the expression of this complex ambiguity.

Unfortunately, the loss of one aspect of Williams's characterization led to further losses. The music of Varsouviana that sounded at key moments throughout the drama could not function as a symbol of Blanche's haunting guilt and so was a dud. In fact, the whole system of Williams's poetic and tragic symbolism was not understood by the company. In Goncharov's conception there was no place for the Mexican woman, who was one of hell's shadows, chanting, "Flores para los muetos," or for lurid reflections and shadows moving along the wall which had become transparent. The hellish atmosphere of the world where there was no privacy, no escape, was not created at all. Certainly it was not a simple inability of the director to follow the author's poetics. There were real aesthetic differences; Williams's plastic theatre could not be confined within the limits of the Russian realistic and psychological theatre.

If we turn to the script of the play, we can find striking examples. In scene nine, when all of Blanche's hopes for peace and rest are dashed, Mitch tells her, "I've never had a real look at you. Let's turn the light here."[18] He wants to be "just realistic" and tears the paper lantern off the light bulb. Does "realism" help him see the truth about Williams's heroine? What does this truth mean; that she is drunk and is older than she wants to seem? As in *The Glass Menagerie*, Williams emphasizes his frightened heroine's preference for soft light to harsh daylight or electric bulbs. Afraid of having her real age revealed, Blanche, like Amanda and Laura, wants to withdraw from the blinding light of reality into the softer world of illusion. Like his heroines, Williams prefers this softer light because it allows him to establish his conception of a plastic theatre where evanescent characters and images flicker across the stage. His dramas cannot stand the blinding light of the realistic theatre and require a different approach and scenic language.

On the Moscow stage, Williams's play and its heroine were also deprived of the author's symbolism "desire versus death." Blanche-Nemolyaeva was not claimed by the opposing forces suggested by two streetcars--Desire and Cemetery. More was involved here than a different aesthetic approach or stage tradition. Goncharov allowed himself cuts that eliminated, whenever it was possible, the rush of sensual and sexual feelings pervasive not only in this play but in all Williams's writing. There was nothing pathological in Nemolyaeva-Blanche, not a hint of her on-going attraction to young boys nor of her dissolute behavior. Nemolyaeva's heroine indeed went through her "intimacies with strangers;" nothing was changed in the plot--but she was made to seem entirely a victim of the brutal world. As I suggested earlier, probably the duality and contradiction in Williams's Blanche could not be interpreted in the traditional psychological manner. She has no way to escape from her past, but, at the same time, her past cannot explain her present deterioration. She is not driven to her present fragmentation by the brutality of the world or by the tragedy of her marriage. That is why Nemolyaeva portrayed a sexless image, poetic, refined, and pitiful. There were none of the dualities or contradictions that Williams had in mind. According to the interpretation of Goncharov and his actress, love for Blanche meant only psychological concord, tenderness, and respect for private relationships in a world where all ties were brittle and accidental.

Of course Goncharov wanted his production to be staged. He realized that it could very easily be deprived of its right to life because of "amorality" and sexual themes. Naturally he wanted to avoid such an outcome. He saw the play in terms of a dichotomy of poetry and refinement versus common prose and vulgarity and he staged it accordingly.

Therefore, according to Goncharov's scheme, Blanche was merely the victim and Stanley committed the atrocities. The part of Stanley was played by Armen Dzhigarkhanyan, a very popular movie and theatre actor. Merciless, streetwise, devoid of sentimentality, his Stanley represented a specific social type--the ruthless, self-satisfied man. His view of life did not encompass any refinement of human nature. Dzhigarkhanyan deliberately created a gloomy and repulsive portrayal, depriving his character of the particular charm and almost animal magnetism given Stanley by the author. It was impossible to imagine Blanche-Nemolyaeva and Stanley-Dzhigarkhanyan feeling sexually drawn to one another. Why did this happen? Why--"in defiance of the play"--was an actor chosen who lacked the physical qualities necessary to portray Stanley? Dzhigarkhanyan was one of the most popular actors in the Mayakovsky; however, the director had a more important reason.

From Goncharov's point of view, it was Williams's intention to condemn Stanley's exultant victory, and the director saw Dzhigarkhanyan as the most suitable choice for meeting his objective. Thus the character of Stanley which should have been complicated and ambiguous, was oversimplified in the Moscow production. Dzhigarkhanyan drew Stanley's image in sharp, vivid, and often straightforward colors. Skillfully, professionally, he played the interpretation of Stanley that Blanche described to her sister--brutal animal and ape.

Dzhigarkhanyan's "super-aim" as Stanley (using Stanislavsky's formulation) was to destroy Blanche. It was his only function and the sole meaning of his scenic existence. Although in Williams's play this is very clear (indeed it is Stanley who forces Blanche toward her last, terrible refuge), Stanley never consciously plots her destruction. Blanche's struggle is surely more with herself than with Stanley; it is not just with "apes" and "brutes" but also with the brutality by which her own moth-like nature is crippled and doomed. Thus there is no triumphant victor in Williams's drama. Stanley does not come out a victor in any contest with Blanche. He just survives; as was the case at Salerno in his "Two-forty-four Engineers" during the war--a survival without victory. Probably Williams wanted us to see that in the modern world, traditions, refinement, and civilization have all become less important than mere survival.

As was the case in the portrayal of Blanche, ambiguity was left out of the director's conception of Stanley. Thus the conflict in Goncharov's production was reduced to the merely external: Stanley's world versus the quest for refinement and inner freedom. However, this external conflict was important enough from the director's point of view, and was also new and important to the Moscow audience. If we take a brief look at the critics' response, Goncharov's innovation in his interpretation of Williams would be more evident.

Yuri Zubkov felt offended. In the article I have cited, "Even in Defiance of the Play," he asked indignantly: "What is the social conflict? What kinds of social forces do Stanley and his friends on the one hand and Blanche on the other personify?" He proceeded to give this answer:

> When it comes to Blanche, the situation is clear: first, owner of a patrimonial estate, then a teacher, and, at the same time half a whore, half a priestess of love. But who are Stanley, Mitch, Pablo, Steve? They are laborers ... They are separate individuals but none of them knows anything except poker, bars and fights. And they are made to personify the American working class.[19]

Another critic, "americanologist" V. Vulf, had a "different" point of view. In his article, "The Tragic Symbolism of Tennessee Williams," published in the principal Soviet theatrical magazine Teatr (Theatre), he called upon critics to judge Williams's plays without oversimplifying and stereotyping. Whereas

Zubkov upbraided the theatre for the lack of social approach, Vulf acknowledged the "serious and thoughtful attitude of a talented artist,"[20] Goncharov. Vulf recognized that Blanche was not only an owner of an estate but also "a representative of the Southern aristocracy."[20] She had no place in modern American society; the time of the Southern aristocracy was gone, and she had to die. Wishing to avoid the "vulgar-sociological" label, Vulf pointed to what he considered as characteristic features of Williams's dramas: the desire of Williams to expose social motives under the limpid cover of psychological conflicts; and the inclination of the playwright to depict "morbid psychology and actions devoid of logic."[20] The critic saw Streetcar as a play about moral insolvency of human personality in a capitalistic society. He was convinced that Williams's intentions were clear: Blanche's loneliness was the result not of her sexual dissoluteness but of social conditions. Blanche and Stanley were social symbols. Blanche was a symbol of the old South, Stanley--of a new "common-man."

Another critic, M. Koreneva in her article, "Passions for Tennessee Williams," looked for the social roots of Stanley's brutality:

> For Williams, connections between this brutality and the fundamental laws of American society are indisputable. But what phenomena are responsible for the use of violence and its continuing rule in that country? Why have violence and ruthlessness become the social norms? It is absolutely useless to try to find in Williams any answers to these important questions.[21]

So concluded Koreneva approaching Williams's drama as if it were a Marxist article on sociology.

We have seen that Goncharov's ideas were different from those of the critics. At a time when critical approach to Williams, Western drama, and indeed to art in general, was mostly gross-sociological like Zubkov's or "without oversimplification and stereotype," as was the case with Vulf, the Moscow director did not want to see Williams's characters as "representatives" of social forces or to look for a Marxist explanation for the dramatic action. Unfortunately, the company allowed itself an inadmissibility. At the conclusion of the play, Mitch was directed to rescue the unconscious Blanche from the Nurse and the Doctor. He carried her away up a short flight of stairs leading to a road that rushed upwards. It is hardly possible to understand what drove Goncharov to change (or to "improve"?) the end of Williams's play.

Probably if the external plot were to be considered from the point of view of a traditional, realistic theatre, this conclusion might appear logical to a director. Mitch, acted in this production by Okhlupin, was a more complex figure than he appeared at first glance. He was plain and natural, confident and truthful, almost humdrum. But after the last conversation with Blanche, he left the stage worried and perplexed. Okhlupin interpreted his part as that of an unhappy lover and produced a strong impression on the audience. He was the only one who felt that Blanche was defenseless in a world of brutality and violence. Perhaps in a classical drama this character might have saved the persecuted heroine. However, there was no escape in Williams's play. Blanche was not crazier in her last scene than she was in the first; she could no longer stand reality and thus had to chose the refuge of madness. This poetics was alien to Goncharov, and so he created the final mise-en-scene which was expressive in itself, but silly and preposterous in relation to the play as a whole.

In 1974, the director of the Berlin Theatre die Freie Volksbuhne had made some deliberate changes when he produced Streetcar. Stanley was played by a black actor and the character of Eunice, as well as the first scene, was eliminated. When Williams heard about this production, he sent a telegram of protest through his agency. There was a court case, and the opening was prohibited for some time. In contrast, Williams never knew what damage--aesthetic and artistic--was done to his play on the Moscow stage. The officials of the Soviet theatre remain unaware of the juridical limitations upon the translation, alteration, and displacement of a play such as this.

With the Goncharov "amendment," the play has continued until now, demonstrating to the audience that kindness and nobility still exist in our world. In Soviet theatres, as in many European theatres, there is the repertoire system, and some productions regularly, a few times a month, appear on the stage over the course of many years. Streetcar still lives in the Mayakovsky theatre with almost the original cast. It has outlived itself, and is now nothing more than a monument to its own self--the first significant attempt at the translation and realization of Williams on the Soviet stage.

More than ten years after the opening of Streetcar, Goncharov again turned to Williams; and in 1982 he staged Cat on a Hot Tin Roof--a consistent production in its own way (with Nemolyaeva as May and Dzhigarkhanyan as Big Daddy). The lessons of Streetcar were not wasted. But for the audience of the early seventies, Streetcar was not something merely for future analyzing; it was an event of historical importance. Even today, when Goncharov's interpretation may be seen as both traditional and preposterous--the tickets are always sold out.

NOTES

14 Tennessee Williams, *A Streetcar Named Desire*, in *Eight Plays*, by Tennessee Williams (New York: Nelson Doubleday, 1982), p. 95. All Williams's plays, with the exception of *Kingdom of Earth*, will be cited from this edition.

15 Tennessee Williams, *A Streetcar Named Desire*, p. 140.

16 Quot. in V. Vulf, "Tragicheskaya Simvolika Tennessi Uilyamsa," *Teatr*, No. 12 (1971), str. 60. (V. Vulf, "The Tragic Symbolism of Tennessee Williams," *Theatre*, p. 60).

17 Quot. in V. Vulf, "Tragicheskaya Simvolika Tennessi Uilyamsa," str. 61.

18 Tennessee Williams, *A Streetcar Named Desire*, p. 177.

19 Quot. in V. Vulf, "Tragicheskaya Simvolika Tennessi Uilyamsa," str. 61.

20 V. Vulf, "Tragicheskaya Simvolika Tennessi Uilyamsa," str. 68.

21 M. Koreneva, "Strasti po Tennessi Uilyamsu," *Teatr*, No. 8 (1971), str. 24. (M. Koreneva, "Passions for Tennessee Williams," *Theatre*, p. 24).

CHAPTER III

THE ENDLESS JOURNEY: COMPREHENDING WILLIAMS

THE GLASS MENAGERIE ON THE SOVIET STAGE

Several years after Williams's first and only book of translated plays was published in the Soviet Union and seven years after Anisimova-Vulf's pitiful attempt to "try Williams" on the Moscow stage, the Moscow Ermolova Theatre was allowed to produce The Glass Menagerie. Why was this particular play of Williams chosen? It was 1969. The so called "socialist-realistic" approach was still the main artistic criterion; one of the greatest tragic and poetic plays in modern theatre was perceived primarily as a critical depiction of ruthless life in capitalistic America. Yet only thirteen years after this production, in the winter of 1982, the same play was staged in Leningrad. This time it was true Williams-- complex, ambiguous, and poetic. It seemed as if, between 1969 and 1982, the whole century had passed.

In this chapter I will attempt to trace the evolution of attitudes and approaches to modern Western drama (to Williams, in particular). I will review, chronologically, five productions of The Glass Menagerie produced over the course of thirteen years in the capital and in the provinces, emphasizing the difficulties encountered by the Soviet stage as it attempted to gain a comprehension of Williams's art.

Despite the fact that the Ermolova's production of The Glass Menagerie was the first one, it was not a major event. N. Abalkin, critic for the Teatralnaya Khronika (Theatre Chronicle), wrote:

> One cannot help noticing how faithful Kaarin Rayad, director, and Lalevich and Sosunov, set designers, have been to Williams; how cleverly and subtly they have conveyed his artistic intention: to portray the far from respectable everyday life of an average American.22

V. Lakirev played the role of Tom as a version of an "angry young man." His hero was angry with American reality. He wanted to be free, to wander, to make verses, but instead he had to work for pennies at The

Continental Shoe Company. That was all that was understood about the tormented Williams's character.

Rayad (the director) designed the part of Laura in such a way that this great poetic role was reduced to naturalism, almost to a pathological case study. The girl who was, according to Williams, "like a piece of translucent glass touched by light,"[23] became physically and emotionally deficient. Despite the fact that H. Vasilieva was a good actress, Laura was not among her best roles. Excessive attention was focused on Laura's lameness.

In this production the only person who tried to convey Williams's complexity was E. Kirillova, the actress who played Amanda. Her intonations--which evoked a dentist's drill--serve to drive not only Tom but also the audience crazy. She was not afraid of thickening comic colors; a ridiculous scarecrow dressed in a thirty-year-old ball gown, wearing a mother's heavy heart on her sleeve. Kirillova liked to play her part close to the proscenium; she felt the necessity of close-ups to reveal the contradiction between her voice and manner and her desperate, fixed stare. She wanted to convince the audience of the deep truth of her feelings and sufferings.

Kirillova's best scene--when the long-awaited gentleman caller revealed that he was not suitable as a fiance for Laura--was called by the critic "The Family Waterloo." There was an outburst of hysterical swearing followed by a lengthy pause and then the same long, desperate stare over the footlights. Pulkhretudova called it "the persecuted Charlie's stare from the early Chaplin films."[24]

Kirillova's acting manner might be defined as "everyday grotesque." The roots of this style, in many respects traditional in the Russian theatre, originated with the MXAT (Moscow Artistic Academic Theatre) and Stanislavsky. We can trace this style to the "pre-historical" studio period of the Ermolova Theatre; to Nikolai Khmelev's striving to distinguish the principal and fundamental essence of the role via the technique of the close-up; to the combining of a "role's garish outer drawing" with "originality of a character's inner world"[25] as Maria Knebel used to remember it. Both Khmelev and Knebel were students of Stanislavsky and among the best actors of the Soviet theatre, as well as leading actors of the MXAT.

"Everyday grotesque" was the best way to create a tragicomic mood, a subtle alloy of the funny and the sad. Kirillova's idea was to use this acting style to portray her heroine, who was both ridiculous and suffering. However, Ermolova's production as a whole was not innovative. Kirillova's personal attempt to convey Williams's heroine could not be given proper development, confined as it was within a "socialist-realistic" dramatic conception.

In speaking of artistic development, one always has to consider both objective and subjective factors. Objective factors include time and its aesthetics, ideological pressure, and international relations. Subjective factors important in the theatrical world are the manoeuvring for careers and the influence of pride and vanity. Kaarin Rayad came to Moscow from Estonia. The cultural history of the Baltic Republics has always been comparatively free-spirited, even within the bounds of Soviet socialism. The Baltic stage was the first to be open to Brecht and other Western playwrights, so Rayad, as a theatrical person, probably had a background of understanding and appreciation of Western art. But The Glass Menagerie in the Ermolova Theatre happened to be her debut in the state capital; here the director's conception had to be beyond any suspicious doubts and conform to the accepted view.

However, this Moscow Menagerie--successful or not--established a sort of official blessing for provincial theatres, and this sanction was broadened after the Mayakovsky production of Streetcar. In 1971, The Glass Menagerie was staged in Perm by E. Lifson as director and it came to Moscow the same year. The Perm theatre made an attempt to convey the complexity and poetry of Williams's great play. Tom, a poet ground down by the realities of American life (a stereotype of the Ermolova production) was moved to a secondary position in the play; Laura's role was made primary.

Laura was played by Svetlana Boldareva. In this production, her spirituality and her inability to confront the outer world became more important issues than her lameness. Her very appearance helped to create the portrait: a clear, almost luminous profile, and bitter wrinkles near the mouth. She had bright, clever eyes, hands entangled in an old shawl and the limp of an injured bird. She was so unlike another character whom Boldareva played at the same time: Luciana from *The Comedy of Errors*--sly, mocking, easy-going, graceful in her splendid dresses, born for admiration. The actress endowed all her heroines with a special charm. There was no single, striking characteristic like infectious laughter that won you at once; she caught you gradually like a hardly noticeable smile. There were delicate and subtle colors in her palette; she liked light lines. None of Boldareva's characters exhausted her range, nor did she ever consider their development as complete. Throughout the productions, she kept adding new features to the portraits. As Laura, Boldareva played all-forgiveness and submissiveness, and yet, at the same time, pride and inability to compromise. There was something of Russian madonnas and saints in her Laura.

In some respects, the Laura on the Perm stage was not the Laura from Williams's play. Boldareva combined extreme vulnerability with an overly sensitive understanding of reality. In spite of this understanding, however, she allowed hope for a miracle. This sense of hope was alien to Williams's Laura, who was completely absorbed in her fragile dream world-- "inside illusion" as Tom put it. She did not see reality at all, and her only reaction to it was nausea. One of Williams's own favorite heroines, Laura, an almost unreal being from the world of her tiny glass figures, symbol of purity and fragility--was in some respects, incomprehensible to the Russian theatre. It understood her in terms of Chekhov. Laura-Boldareva rather resembled one of the *Three Sisters*, who existed somewhere between the cruel reality she saw and comprehended and the cherished illusion to escape: "To Moscow! To Moscow!"

When the miracle did happen, and the "Prince Charming" arrived in the form of an ordinary clerk, the blue color began intensifying on the stage. There was pale blue on Laura's dress and victorious blue on Jim's coat. Dramatic blue candles were on the tables. (One is reminded of Blanche Du Bois, on her last evening, wearing a blue jacket. "Della Robbia Blue," she explains. "The blue of the robe in the old Madonna pictures.")[26] The stage-director in Perm presumed that the blue color alone could symbolically produce all the complexity of feeling associated with Laura as she turned into "Blue Rose." Williams's symbolism was comprehended too literally, and as a result looked merely, superficially illustrative.

Jim, as played by V. Ginzburg, was an ambitious character in love with himself. "Look, what a big shadow I have."[27] He said that line as if bewitched by his own image and devoid of any sense of humor. In many respects, he and Amanda remained characters designed to expose and convict the vulgar reality of American life. However, Ginzburg gave his hero an ability to see in Laura the poetry of "Blue Rose" and to favor her with a precious moment of happiness.

Amanda, as played by L. Mossolova, was closer to one of Ostrovsky's merchant's wives from nineteenth century Russia than she was to a modern American lady. She portrayed a woman of uncertain age, who tried to conceal her years by cosmetics and belatedly girlish, mincing manners. She did not want to accept the fact that her youth and beauty were gone and all her hopes were futile. She was narrow-minded and vulgar. She had a kind of strength to survive in any environment because only the outer surface of her being came into contact with reality. Her "glass menagerie," her memories and fantasies, were insulated from any outer influences; here she was invulnerable.

The very stage existence of Mossolova's Amanda seemed consciously artificial. She did not even speak in a full range of tones but employed only her highest register, as if keeping the rest of her voice in reserve for a special emergency. In the Perm production, this emergency came just once. In the scene when Amanda realized that Jim was engaged to another girl, Mossolova gave a fearful performance of downfall. Her Amanda struggled to remain courteous, but right before the eyes of the audience her protective coats of both make-up and manners seemed to fade away. She suddenly grew enfeebled and flabby as if struck by a blow, and she aged instantly.

In the Perm theatre, the direction might have been defined as actor-oriented as opposed to spectacle-oriented. The actor was trained to develop the ability to live through the perception of a separate human being. He had to find, inside himself, the kernel that could give rise to one more distinctive stage character. The problem with this production was that the technique did not fit the dramatic material. Williams requires a certain degree of relativity, alienation, and the ability of the actor to create a symbolic existence in a painful dream-world. Instead we were given the realistic transformation of an actor into his character.

As we have seen, Mossolova's portrayal of Amanda was different in nature from Kirillova's in the Ermolova theatre. Mossolova's Amanda was a practical, full-blooded woman, who lived in very different world from that grotesque place inhabited by Kirillova's suffering heroine. However, in general this Perm production was an attempt to see in The Glass Menagerie something more than a simple condemnation of American life. The comprehension of new drama, or, in broader terms, theatrical development as a whole, seldom looks like pure progression; what was a step forward in one case could prove to be a step backward in another. But for the Soviet theatre the most important fact was that exploration had begun and not in vain, for nothing is really wasted in the world of theatre.

When in 1975 this play was produced in the city of Ivanovo (near Moscow), the main purpose was to concentrate on the timeless and universal, on poetry and beauty, on illusion as it is opposed to reality. This was the vision of director L. Vaynstein, and fortunately lyricism did not turn to sentimentality; compassion never became maudlin. The theatre tried to search out the dramatic sources for the characters and their destinies. But in this projection of the past upon the present there was no emotional redundancy, as there had been in the two earlier productions. What was enacted on the Ivanovo stage was not a stream of realistic life but events selected by memory and filtered by time.

For Tom Wingfield re-experiencing his youth, the past possessed a great deal of something enduring. In this production, the tiny, fragile figures of the glass menagerie became the symbols not only of purity but also of broken dreams, lost illusions. This theme of lost illusions was considered by the director to be the principal one. He stressed the similarities between the characters. Even the Father was interpreted as the victim of his own romantic illusions. In this production he was more than an invisible presence; his portrait was literally suspended over the Wingfield's living room like some kind of fate hanging over the house.

Enlarging the mise-en-scenes the director re-constituted the image of Time. The web ceiling became a symbol of oblivion as Tom narrated incidents of his own life; or it might be seen as representing the suffocation of the everyday routine in which he had taken part. The director wanted to remove Tom's romantic veil: to cast doubt on his poetic vocation. Vaynstein did not see Tom as a creative, Orpheus-like figure who descended into the dark depth of his subconsciousness to create art out of his own poignant memories. Brought up in the classical traditions of Russian realistic and psychological theatre, the Ivanovo company saw in Tom's flight from home primarily a flight from himself and also the repudiation of his responsibilities for those who were near and dear. This conception of an angry, rebellious Tom was better suited to the actor, Michael Asaphov, than was the interpretation of Williams's hero as suffering poet, creating a play from the ashes of his destroyed past, a play at once memory and something he wished he could forget. Asaphov-Tom was a grown-up, experienced man who lacked those poignant reflections that mix bitterness and grief.

Asaphov-Tom dealt with his anguish by cherishing the fond illusion to escape. For his sister, Laura (actress T. Garkusha), existence in an illusory world was organic and natural. In this production, Laura's life was a gradual and irreversible withdrawal from outer reality, until she was flung into the abyss of final and irreparable despair.

Jim O'Connor (actor V. Zhukovsky) and Amanda Wingfield (actress V. Krasnoslobodskaya) turned out to be surprisingly related figures in this performance. The director saw the psychological orientation of these two characters as similar: both could adapt to changing circumstances; both could play the game of making party conversation; both were nostalgically intoxicated with their own pasts.

However, the Russian theatre's understanding of the past and Williams's perception of the past as myth were and had to be different. The author described Amanda as "a little woman ... clinging frantically to another time and place."[28] Amanda's past, for Williams, not only animated but also sustained her in the present, becoming her point of reference for all goodness, truth, and reality. The present, on the other hand, existed for her only to the degree it could be verified by constant reference to the Southern past. Williams employed the South of history and myth as an image that mediated between what was and what might be.

It was a myth that was highly significant for Williams and for those of his characters trapped in the past, or in an imaginary "lost" time. It was a way to escape time and history.

For the Russian stage, with its realistic and psychological traditions, the mythological way of thinking was not only incomprehensible but absolutely alien. As usual, a character's past was seen--not as something mythical and universal, but as real biography that had formed him as a social type and could therefore explain his present attitudes.

The Ivanovo theatre saw the future in terms of Amanda's and Jim's past success. Whether this promise was illusory or real, one had to believe in it. That was why the major role of Jim, Zhukovsky in this production, was to convince Laura that "to be disappointed in life is one thing but to give up hoping is another."[29] This was not the direct translation of the original script, but the theatre needed to put it that way. Jim's monologue, though addressed to the credulous Laura, sounded like an attempt at self-persuasion. It was the way Jim reinforced his belief in his own abilities.

Krasnoslobodskaya played Amanda as a woman who, though distinctive in her own right, combined in her personality some features of each of the other characters. She had Jim's optimism, Laura's lyricism, and she shared Tom's quest for a romantic life. But every character's stage life centered on a major theme. Amanda's theme, according to Williams, was the memory of her youth. For the actress, Amanda's mythical past was less important than her present--mother, suffering, despotic, devoting herself to her children and excessively demanding. Her portrayal wavered between spiritual extremes; her cheerfulness could suddenly turn into inconsolable despair; childish unsophistication easily gave way to callousness or even cruelty. In a family of sufferers, Amanda suffered the most, both because of her impoverished destiny and because of her belief that this ridiculous fate would necessarily be relived by her children. Amanda became paralyzed at the end. She saw her attempts to initiate change in her family life as comic and preposterous.

By the mid-seventies, the vulgar-sociological approach to art was not so dominant on the Soviet stage as it had been in the sixties. Thus the Ivanovo production was freer from misinterpretation and oversimplification, freer to search seriously for a true understanding of American drama.

As we have seen, on the Soviet stage this search was conducted simultaneously in two directions: in the traditional channel of psychological drama and in the new direction of ambiguity and symbolism. And when The Glass Menagerie came back to Moscow in 1980, a considerable step forward was taken in comprehending Williams's ideas and his plastic theatre. It was staged this time by L. Levertov in the TYUZ (Theatre of a Young Spectator--Teatr Yunogo Zritelya). Both the theatre and its audience had come a long way since the Ermolova production of 1969 with its anger at American reality. By the early eighties, Tennessee Williams had become one of the best known, most popular and most frequently performed of Western playwrights. Many of his plays were being given on various Moscow stages: Orpheus Descending, Sweet Bird of Youth, Kingdom of Earth, A Streetcar Named Desire. The Soviet theatre had begun to feel more comfortable with the symbolic and ambiguous elements of Williams's art.

Levertov proclaimed the genre of his production to be "sentimental tragedy." He wanted the audience to be constantly reminded that they were watching reminiscences, and he conveyed the action in a nostalgic haze. His aim was "to convey the invisible and to outline the incredible." He felt that there would only be truth "if mystery were surrounded by the objects of everyday life."30

Stage designer V. Talalay dressed the stage in plain, colorless, simply draped cloths. They could easily reflect the soft and tender lights of lilac, orange, amber and blue. The action was centered on a rotating stage, and the mood was tempered by its smooth and gradual movements, no matter what tragedies underlined the scene. Since all tragedies belonged to the past, the audience saw only memories of them. The peaceful mood so characteristic of this production and so beautifully executed, intensified the spectators' sense of the "quiet mysteries of life" (Chekhov) and made the play look more like one of Chekhov than one of Williams. There was something concert-like about the atmosphere of that production; in fact, a violinist appeared on the stage from time to time playing etudes --an unnecessarily decorative and naive touch. The imposition of such "poetization" was annoying, although it could not influence the performance in general.

The actor V. Platonov as Tom was directed to concentrate on the nostalgic aspect of the role, the one beyond the plot. Tom's attitude toward his mother--a very complex aspect of his part--was the most interesting thing in Platonov's performance. This wiser Tom looked at Amanda from the outside, from the position of lonely freedom, already aware that the quest for freedom could only lead to separation. Thus, in his memories, Tom watched his mother in a lyrical mood, without any trace of bitterness or irritation. The suffering poet unable to resist his calling had disappeared from the TYUZ production. Although the figure of a poet who paradoxically becomes a liar and destroyer was important to Williams, it was not important to Levertov's performance with its Chekhovian mood.

Clearly this Moscow <u>Glass Menagerie</u> reflected Chekhov's tradition of Russian theatre: everyday life with its own subtle poetry was being reproduced on the stage, even though it happened through the process of memory. People were dining, going to the movies, talking endlessly, crying, quarreling and loving one another. Behind all this, of course, tragedies were hidden--tragedies of disappointment, disillusionment, lost hopes.

L. Knyaseva played an Amanda forced to hope for the success of the visit of the Gentleman Caller but all too aware of the inevitability of its failure. However, she was not a nervous or paranoiac lady; nor was she overwhelmed by her loneliness or by her heart-breaking family troubles. ("She is not a paranoiac, but her life is paranoia,"[31] Williams had remarked). Employing strict rhythms, Knyaseva looked like an old-fashioned school teacher, sure of herself and well aware of what she must do. A very important aspect of this image had disappeared completely: the grotesque or eccentric quality with its own kind of tragic poetry. The very first Soviet Amanda, Kirillova, had tried this approach in the Ermolova Theatre. However, the banal and tedious character of this Amanda could better account for the reticence and seclusion of her children. For both director and actress, the tragi-comic and arrogant matriarchy was logical; it was based on their perception of a haughty Southern lady.

The Southern myth, a myth of aristocracy and

nobility of spirit, had provided Williams's Amanda with images of youth, love and purity--all ideals that had disappeared along with mansions and family fortunes. But to Levertov and the Moscow TYUZ this myth centered on the sweet triumphs of an extravagant, whimsical and wealthy young woman who invited the adoration of innumerable wealthy admirers. Although Williams's Amanda saw herself as an Aphrodite with jonquils surrounded by multiple analogues of Adonis in a kind of Dionysian meadow, the company gave a different interpretation of the past that determined and sharpened the pretensions of Knyaseva-Amanda. She was harsh and peremptory with her children, as the director assumed her to have been with the lovers in her past.

This interpretation of Amanda is better understood in the light of Russian stage tradition, which requires an actor in a realistic and psychological drama to create a type: a typical character in typical circumstances. In order to make his theatrical existence truthful, an actor tried to justify psychologically--for himself and the audience--every spiritual and physical moment of his character. Thus if Amanda had come from a wealthy family and were accustomed to being treated as a queen, that past had to be reflected--in plastic and in intonation--in the stage type.

Actress T. Abduchanova appeared in this production as a self-apologetic Laura. Shy and colorless, she made no claims. Boldareva's Laura in the Perm production, with her strong sense of reality, was unacceptable to the TYUZ director. He understood Williams's heroine as the one who lacked feelings for the outer world. Reality had no positive meaning for Laura-Abduchanova, and after the departure of the Gentleman Caller, its clear outlines were lost completely. At the end of the performance, Laura was silent and sad as she sat by the pink candle among the animals of her tiny glass menagerie. This plastic image seemed to have originated in the classic Russian ballet--an unrealized Giselle. But one felt that the silhouetted, transparent figures could not warm any human soul for long. The past was merging into darkness, dissolving in memory and time--beautifully and sentimentally.

Utilizing plastic images, color and lighting, the Moscow TYUZ had made a serious attempt to capture the fragile world of The Glass Menagerie. However, due to the strong traditions of the Russian stage, the process of comprehending Williams was neither smooth nor easy. If we examine one more production, an interesting work in itself, we may have a clearer picture of the development of this process.

The Glass Menagerie was staged by Geta Yanovska in the Leningrad MDT (Little Drama Theatre--Maly Dramatichesky Teatr) at the end of 1982. Since modern American and English drama made up almost half of the MDT repertory, it was obviously an appropriate place for Williams. Hemingway's *Fiesta*, *Incident* by Nicolas E. Baer were performed here as was Shelagh Delaney's *A Taste of Honey* (the latter was the first production of Geta Yanovska and has been performed successfully for more than ten years). In fact, Williams's *Rose Tattoo* had already been given a powerful staging by Leo Dodin, the MDT's artistic director, an artist gifted with a mythological and universal way of thinking. Thus Williams was not a chance encounter either for the MDT or for Geta Yanovska, whose husband, Kama Ginkas, had, in 1978, staged what may have been the best Soviet production of Williams--*Kingdom of Earth*--at the Leningrad Theatre on Liteiny Prospekt.

The whole atmosphere of Geta Yanovska's *Glass Menagerie* was different from the lyrical, nostalgic Moscow TYUZ production. Like light penetrating tiny glass figures, it had a trembling, nervous quality. Tom, played by the interesting and talented young actor Victor Gvozdisky, sounded the basic note of anxiety. For the actor, this role had an autobiographical meaning. When still in high school, Gvozdisky had run away from his small-town home to devote himself to the theatre, in defiance of his parents. At this point in time, he had already graduated from the Theatre Department, and had been playing roles noticed by the critics; still his parents waited for their prodigal son to seek out a "normal" career. The actor's resulting feelings of guilt were of major importance for his penetration into the character of Tom.

Two mise-en-scenes in Yanovska's *Menagerie*--both portrayals of Tom's attempts to escape--were of special importance for this production as a whole. Tom's departure at the end, when, smashing his glass on the floor, he caused Laura to scream in fright, was reminiscent of his earlier attempt to run away. Calling Amanda an "ugly-old-witch," he had ripped off his coat, thrown it across the room, shattering some of

Laura's glass menagerie. She had cried out as if wounded. The symbolism was obvious: Tom could not escape without shattering Laura's fragile self; he could not abandon his past without destroying it. If only he could model his life as did others! His mother was able to live in the mythical past. His sister found a poetry in the tiny glass figures. His father, with "Hello-Good-bye," had disappeared into a new life. But the destiny of Gvozdisky's hero was the everlasting torture of breaking-off and returning. That is why in Yanovska's production the stairs were very important: just as Tom "took off," we could hear the crashing sound of his rough boots as he "flew" down.

This Tom possessed a sound knowledge of his own treachery, which Yanovska indicated using symbolism of light and darkness. When Tom, instead of paying the light bill, used the money on his dues to the merchant marine, shadows fell across the stage for the first time. At the end, when he directed Laura to blow out the candles, the darkness became complete. The most important thing for Tom-Gvozdisky, the meaning of his stage existence, was to leave his haunting memories "behind," to plunge them into everlasting darkness.

In this production, the portiere curtain provided a dividing line on the stage between illusion and reality, or between one kind of truth and another. Most of the time Gvozdisky played his part standing at the portiere, as if trying to keep his distance. From the start he appeared to be on the way out. However, at the end it was clear that no such way existed for him: neither for the actor inside illusion, nor for the narrator or playwright speaking from outside. The play is memory, according to Tom, but Gvozdisky's hero created this play in order to forget. He has been the only Tom on the Russian stage capable of living in two worlds at the same time. Gvozdisky portrayed the "angry young man" with bitter and nostalgic memories, the character patterned after the previous productions. But in addition Gvozdisky-Tom played a double game in this theatre: he was both the narrator of the play and the character within it; both "the emissary from the world of reality" and a man whose life was bounded by what he --as narrator--called "truth in the pleasant disguise of illusion."

Gvozdisky as Tom was caught between the past and the present and his hero rejected both of them. Tom Wingfield re-created his haunting past in a dim and poetic atmosphere, where plastic movements of Gvozdisky's character seemed uneasy and anxious and his intonations were sometimes broken and affected. The concept of Gvozdisky's plasticity was designed to be non-realistic and theatrical, to express simultaneously the life of the body and of the spirit. His Tom was, first of all, a poet, a suffering creator, who tried to persuade the audience and himself that human tragedy was nothing but "the play, play, play!" But who knows for sure where illusion and artistic creation end and reality begins?

Tom Wingfield was not the first poet portrayed by Gvozdisky. He had previously acted the part of the great Russian poet Alexander Pushkin. It was an experimental one-man performance, <u>Pushkin</u> <u>and</u> <u>Natali</u>, staged by Kama Ginkas (the husband of Yanovska) in the Young Actor's Workshop of the Leningrad Theatre Society. There was no stage. The young man dressed in blue jeans and sweater stood near the audience in a small room. He was accompanied by a portrait of Natali (Pushkin's wife), wedding flowers, a candle, a pack of playing cards, and a pile of letters to various addressees--the bride, the bride's mother, friends, enemies, and a chief of gendarmes. What did all of them --the cards, the flowers, and the letters--have in common? They belonged to the same person. However, it was never enough to create a unity for the work of art. As Leo Tolstoy noted, this unity could only come "from the author's distinctive moral attitude for the subject."[32] Amidst the confusion of the letters, Gvozdisky nonetheless caught the concrete reality-- the life of Pushkin as he lived it and as others viewed it. He captured as well a unique plasticity-- from the serious, almost tragic, to the humorous; from everyday routine to the defense of honor; from blunt openness to constrained politeness; from the soul's outcry to a sense of bitter irony. One state of the soul blended into another with no marked divisions, no abrupt transitions. Taken as a whole his portrayal was a unique creation.

Gvozdisky did the same kind of thing in <u>The Glass Menagerie</u>. He created a field of enormous tension. He managed to exist in two different worlds simultaneously --in the domestic hell of the Wingfields and in the tormented reality of his everlasting returns to it. These two worlds together provided the material for artistic creation.

Yanovska staged a production about a suffering poet pursued by the furies of his own feelings of guilt; the MDT <u>Glass Menagerie</u> appeared to be a play written for and about one character. Laura (O. Belyavska), Amanda (V. Bukova), and Jim (M. Samochko) were just Tom's assistants, his artistic creations. The four made a very good ensemble, but the independent tragic meaning of Laura's and Amanda's parts were missing.

The director brought a new character into this production: the Father. From time to time he would appear on the stage, sometimes repeating lines after his wife and children, revealing more completely the meaning of what they said, embodying their complicated feelings and attitudes towards himself. Thus he was neither an absent family member who "fell in love with a long distance"[33] and disappeared, nor a photograph coming to life in memories. He was rather the fantasy of a mythical courtship, a dream of freedom and reality. Yanovska felt the necessity for this character because she wanted to stress something which for her was especially important in this play--the cyclical repetition, the acting out again and again of the same single, futile pattern. The Father began it. His only words that we know are contained in the brief message of the picture postcard, "Hello-Goodbye!" The MDT saw in these words an ironic summary of the play's pattern of anticipation, brief fulfillment and subsequent loss and disillusion. In the Leningrad production Williams's play turned into a ritual of losses, and the sense of loss and despair was overwhelming. The poet was forced to exist and to create in a universe not merely indifferent but actually hostile to human fate.

Thus we have seen a development from the "realistic" picture of an "average American" way of life to the Poet's tragedy in a world of loss and despair, the outcome of twelve years in the life of <u>The Glass Menagerie</u> on the Soviet stage. The fact that this play had a previous forty-year theatrical history did not make it easier to realize in the Soviet Union where the process of comprehending and staging Williams was so complicated. We have seen how ideological conditions determined the transformation of <u>The Glass Menagerie</u> into a flat criticism of "cruel" American reality. However, even in this first production, there were the seeds of a true achievement and they marked the beginning of a serious artistic search. In spite of different theatrical and cultural traditions, Tennessee Williams has become an author of a spiritual necessity for the Soviet stage. The process of comprehending his dramas has been on-going, as we have seen in the example of <u>The Glass Menagerie</u>. Despite unevenness and inevitable mistakes, ideological control notwithstanding, this process will continue. The best Soviet <u>Glass Menagerie</u> is yet to come. But as Peter Brook has said, "We begin a journey which has no end, but for the true artist the journey itself is the real reward."[34]

NOTES

22 N. Abalkin, "Steklyanny Zverinets v Teatre imeni Ermolovoy," Teatralnaya Khronika, No. 12 (1975), str. 31. (N. Abalkin, "The Glass Menagerie in the Ermolova Theatre," Theatre Chronicle, p. 31).

23 Tennessee Williams, The Glass Menagerie, p. 55.

24 E. Pulkhretudova, "Ermolovtsy: Sezony Proshlye i Nyneshnie," Teatr, No. 8 (1969), str. 20. (E. Pulkhretudova, "The Ermolova Theatre: the Past and the Present," Theatre, p. 20).

25 P. Markov, V Moskovskom Khudozhestvennom Akademicheskom Teatre (Moskva: VTO, 1976), str. 431. (P. Markov, In the Moscow Artistic Academic Theatre, p. 431).

26 Tennessee Williams, A Streetcar Named Desire, p. 191.

27 It is interesting that this was the way the company interpreted the original line: "Look, I'm in the limelight." (The Glass Menagerie, p. 71).

28 Tennessee Williams, The Glass Menagerie, p. 7.

29 The original line is: "Being disappointed is one thing and being discouraged is another. I'm disappointed but I'm not discouraged." (p. 76).

30 A. Inyakhin, "Trudnye Deti Uzhasnykh Roditeley," Teatr, No. 9 (1980), str. 19. (A. Inyakhin, "The Problem Children of the Terrible Parents," Theatre, p. 19).

31 Tennessee Williams, The Glass Menagerie, p. 7.

32 L. N. Tolstoy o Literature i Iskusstve (Moskva: Sovremennik, 1978), str. 30. (L. N. Tolstoy about Literature and Art, p. 30).

33 Tennessee Williams, The Glass Menagerie, p. 40.

34 Peter Brook, The Empty Space (London, 1968), p.32.

CHAPTER IV

ORPHEUS CASTRATED: ORPHEUS DESCENDING AND SWEET BIRD OF YOUTH ON THE MOSCOW STAGES

The so-called "violent" plays of Tennessee Williams do not have a long history on the Soviet stage. Suddenly Last Summer has never been translated and staged. Sweet Bird of Youth and Orpheus Descending, however, were done in Moscow, almost at the same time. Sweet Bird was performed at the MXAT (Moscovsky Khudozhestvenny Akademichesky Teatr--Moscow Artistic Academic Theatre) in 1975 and Orpheus at the TTSA (Tsentralny Teatr Sovetskoy Armii--The Central Theatre of the Soviet Army) in 1977. In spite of the success of these plays, Soviet provincial theatres have never had the courage to stage them.

These Williams's dramas, "as violent as you can get on the stage,"[35] as the author said of them in his "Foreword" to Sweet Bird, were too intimidating for the Soviet theatre. The years of the Russian Williams experience have made it clear that the major function of Williams's symbols is to form an emotional bridge with the audience. His symbols create a drama so emotionally charged with archetypal images that their realization make the particular general, the strange familiar, and even the grotesque recognizable as another dimension of the human condition. The hell created by Williams out of the American South can be perceived as the condition of the human being in general and under a totalitarian system in particular. The figures of Boss Finley and Jabe Torrance, the agents by which hell annihilates everyone dissimilar and everyone disliked, can easily remind us of the recent past. Their clique, as well as the other inhabitants of Two River County or St. Cloud who have thoroughly learned the self-righteous "truths" hammered into their sluggish, narrow minds, can be very familiar. Their "truths" deal with life and death, rights and law, "ordinary honest men" versus outsiders. Their inclination towards mob psychology can also be frighteningly recognizable.

In spite of that (or perhaps because of that), the minds and imaginations of stage-directors were attracted to Sweet Bird and Orpheus. However, there was one important condition: on the stage hell had to be American. If not, the emphasis would be different.

When, in 1982, in the Leningrad Theatre on Liteiny Prospekt, Yakov Khamarmer, the director, was trying to stage <u>One Flew over the Cuckoo's Nest</u>, the performance was allowed only after the third check-up and approval by Party Officials and only after the American flag was placed conspicuously on both the stage and the sleeves of all the attendants in the asylum. The main hero had to be dressed as a Green Beret. So, when V. Shilovsky in the MXAT and A. Burdonsky in the TTSA were about to stage <u>Sweet Bird</u> and <u>Orpheus</u>, they knew what and whom they had to deal with. They saw the plots as lifelike and very specific. They understood the tense psychological message of the dramas with their murders, lynching, and hunting people down and portrayed them as a reflection of real life in the American South.

In <u>Orpheus</u> and <u>Sweet Bird</u>, as almost everywhere in Williams's plays, there are frenzied figurativeness, the unexpected combination of hell's torments with tragic farce and notes of pure heart-felt lyricism. All that created the view of life as a modern hell to which everyone is condemned. Williams's way of thinking is mythological, and his dramatic myths unite the theatrical relativity with the absolutism of truth. Moscow stage-directors did not venture to think in that scope. They showed Williams psychologically, in a fashion traditional for the Russian stage. In spite of that, these Moscow versions of the American Southern hell were attractive in their seriousness and in their ability to underline the main ideas of the plays.

In the TTSA <u>Orpheus</u>, the set designer, S. Barkhin, was closer to Williams's poetics than was the director. He tried to find the degree of theatrical relativity that could assure both concrete reality and the universality of the myth. In the stage-right corner he placed a high, round table with half-empty wine bottles on it, a few chairs, and the stairway; at stage-left— a bar or a counter. There were not many details specific to the action. Somewhere behind the bar there was Lady's confectionary, unclear to the audience but illuminated by bluish light as a somewhat alluring vista. In the background, the artist omitted the skeleton advised by Williams as a symbol of death. Barkhin needed the figure of a bronze angel as a symbol of the long-awaited salvation that the sufferers in hell hoped for. The slot machines, "one-armed bandits," mentioned by Dog and Pee Wee in the first scene, were placed in the proscenium. Designed as male and female figures, they seemed to be a mutilated and corrupted

Adam and Eve, who had already drained the cup of their earthly suffering to the dregs. The image created by the stage-designer was that of a cold, prisonlike house ("Christ ... It's cold as a goddam ice plant ... I don't know why, it never seems to hold heat," Lady kept saying). The few objects scattered around the stage at a far distance from each other gave the feeling of discomfort, a place where one could hardly breathe.

"I began to feel breathless," again and again repeated Princess Kosmonopolis finding herself in the "blood-thirsty ogre's country" that was created by the artist Boris Messerer on the MXAT stage. There were no modern constructions to startle our imagination. Following the author's directions, Messerer led the audience into a number of different places--the interior of an old, fashionable hotel, the bar in this hotel, or the terrace of the outwardly impressive house of Boss Finley. The artist used smooth curves of the modernist style from the beginning of our century. Somehow on stage, however, the lines assumed rigidness, and the colors, under the lights, became a joyless ochre-brown or a garish crimson. Both lines and colors helped to set the tone of the play--malicious and anti-humane.

However, the directors' conceptions in both productions were not so definite as the stage images of the anti-humane world created by the theatres' set designers. The Moscow versions of <u>Sweet Bird</u> and <u>Orpheus</u> lacked mythical dimensions and universal (as opposed to local, American-Southern) meaning. In part this can be explained by the general complexity of these plays, especially when realized on the Russian stage, traditionally accustomed to psychological and realistic drama. There was also the problem of how, in an ideologically controlled theatre, to show the grinding down of everybody who was different.

In the TTSA, the world created by the director, A. Burdonsky, turned out to be just commonplace. Williams's hell is inhabited by cold, hypocritical creatures--grotesque, provincial Furies--various Dollies and Beulahs with their husbands. These inhabitants of Two River County resemble Faulkner's Yoknapatawpha characters--plunderers, deserters, killers. In the drowsy stupidity of Dog and Pee Wee, the combined Cerberus of this god-forsaken place, there is so much desire to find fun in cruelty, to set dogs on men, and to attack for the sake of attacking that one can forget that they are human. However, on this stage, they did not appear as forces suggestive of totalitarism. Instead they provided a mere background for the action: outer characterizations were substituted for inner meaning. The ominous essence of Sheriff Talbott, inveterate killer "in the name of the law," and that of Jabe Torrance, symbol of an order that sentences and kills, were minimized. Actor M. Mayorov played Jabe, frightful in his ordinariness, but the image did not turn into an incarnation of brutality, as it is in Williams: a human machine that destroys life and inner freedom whenever he finds them.

Likewise, in the MXAT, Boss Finley did not have the appearance of a sinister "beanstalk country" political leader. He was played by Pavel Massalsky, a wonderful and very famous actor. The theme of weariness dominated Massalsky's performance. His Boss was an elderly and not very healthy man whose fatique seemed endless. He was tired of his own impudent demagoguery, and of the necessity to be always in sight of the people he infinitely despised. He was tired of preaching the racial theory of his "sacred mission," in which he had lost faith long ago. But most of all, this Boss Finley seemed sick to death of being a ruler who chastised his subjects. His thoughts were preoccupied by his love for Heavenly and his feelings for Miss Lucy, whose passion he--alas!--was unable to satisfy further. These two women were very important for him, to the exclusion of anything else.

In the context of Massalsky's performance, Tom Junior (artist N. Penkov) was given an unexpected interpretation. Short but well-built, this Tom was not very noticeable among his broad-shouldered and stalwart friends, yet he easily bent them to his will. Even with his father, Tom assumed an independent air and snubbed him on occasion. He had a harsh, piercing glare and was a mass of energy and strength--a true Napoleon of St. Cloud. It was not difficult for one to guess that in the near future this Tom Junior would become, not only an organizer and inspirer (he was in part already), but an official leader of his fascist thugs. The "beanstalk country's" future belonged to him, and this future-- alas!--was of ill omen. However, even with this kind of interpretation, the frightful quality of St. Cloud public life was underplayed.

In neither the TTSA nor the MXAT was Williams's

hell shown to its full extent. As a result, "descending" saviors were deprived of their major meaning. The women, Lady and Princess Kosmonopolis, were placed in the center and became the main heroines of the action.

The stage-director of the TTSA <u>Orpheus</u>, Burdonsky, thought of Lady as the active, consciously rebellious foundation of the play. He and the actress Ludmila Kasatkina led Williams's heroine through sufferings, struggle, love, and death, where her image became majestic and purified of self-interest and materialism. Lady-Kasatkina became the soul of the production. Her acting lacked details and nuances, and her portrayal was roundly, broadly tragic. This Lady was deliberately rough and despotic. In the sweeping, sharp movements and wide gait, in the imperious voice of Jabe Torrance's wife, there were no traces of the former Lady who was tender and open to life and love. Kasatkina intentionally brought the image down. There was neither lyricism, nor spirituality: this Eurydice was too preoccupied with the store she had in Hell and with her daily receipts to worry much about being liberated by Orpheus. Grief and hatred had burned out and trampled the soul of Lady-Kasatkina as the mob had burned out her father. Her features were hidden behind the mask of respectable store-keeper. Yet one was always aware of her nervous tension, and every word or gesture revealed that she was ready to explode. When, for a moment, the mask fell off, there was nothing behind it but hatred and despair. Even her love for Val did not change her outlook. For this Lady, the transformation of her confectionary into the wine garden did not mean rebirth or even the illusion of revived love and youth. The only thing she yearned for was revenge.

Only when she felt she was carrying a new life in her body, did Kasatkina's heroine finally change. Tension left her body, and her face became gentle and feminine. It seemed as if throughout the whole performance, up until this time, Kasatkina had been saving up, cherishing and hiding the light and tenderness. She lighted up, and suddenly the tarantella of her Italian childhood was revived, a tarantella of happiness and challenge that was always met by a great ovation from the audience. This was the dance of Lady-Kasatkina's triumph. Her face showed no fear of death when she saw Jabe Torrance. According to the script, she screamed in fright and retreated haltingly like a blind person. But Kasatkina's heroine met Death, personified by her husband, silently and proudly. She was intrepid and whole-hearted in her gladness, in her suffering, and in her death.

This interpretation and the style of acting was not quite compatible with the unfathomable role created by Williams and previously acted by Anna Magnani. What ideas did Williams connect with the image of Lady and why did they happen to be unacceptable for the Moscow production?

There are three stories of importance for Williams that become an integral part of that modern version of the Orphic myth he created. There is the story of Val as an Orpheus-Dionysius-Christlike figure. There is another one recounted at the beginning by the choral figures, Dolly and Beulah, about Lady, and later retold by Lady herself. Its theme is the youthful love of Lady and David Cutrere, recalled as an idyllic moment of passionate fulfilment in the wine garden of Lady's father. In the midst of Two River County, Papa Romano had attempted to create an earthly paradise with "grapevines and fruit trees," as Lady remembered. It had white, latticed arbors and the couples making love evoked both Adam's and Eve's Edenic bower and the Dionysian wine grove. The ecstatic passion of David and Lady ("those two met like you struck two stones together and a fire! yes ... a fire ... ")36 bears fruit in Lady's conceiving, while the savages of the Mystic Crew burn up the wine garden. The Edenic Unity is ruined. The love story of Lady and David in the orchard is re-enacted, like mythical ritual, by Lady and Val in the artificial restoration of the wine garden, behind a faded Oriental curtain. The curtain bears the design of "a gold tree with scarlet fruit and fantastic birds," the mere facade of an earthly paradise. Their passion also leads to fertility and conception, but ends in death and the fire of a blowtorch.

The fire of love and passion and the fire of death which spread over Williams's play were totally absent from the Moscow production; this Lady's conscious rebellion against evil differed from that envisioned by Williams. His concept of love and passion as uncontrollable elements was unacceptable to Burdonsky. Williams made these symmetrical repetitions of Lady's love story take the majestic form of myth, an archetypal story of anticipation and loss, of expectation and disappointment, of hope and ultimate despair. However, mythical and especially biblical allusions were something impossible for the Soviet stage to realize and would not have been understood by the audience.

Having failed to understand the mythical and ritualistic dimensions of Orpheus, the theatre was also unable to see the necessity of the other two stories so important both for the image of Lady and for the meaning of the play itself. Lady's story of a monkey and her story of a barren tree were considered unnecessary and were simply eliminated.

The first one, the story of an old monkey sold to Papa Romano by a liar who claimed that it was young, is of the utmost importance to the play. It implies the divestment of illusion, the futility of rejuvenation, and the finality of death. The dressed-up monkey danced in the sun. But one day it danced too much, the sun was too hot, the monkey was too old, and it dropped dead. "The show is over," said Lady's father. "The monkey is dead."37 Like this monkey, Lady attempts rejuvenation by going to the beauty parlor and getting all dressed up on the night of the opening of the recreated wine garden. However, it is all artificial, with only the illusion of restoration. Her final dance becomes a dance macabre. Echoing the grim punch line of the monkey's story, the last words of Lady are: "The show is over. The monkey is dead." On the TTSA stage, Kasatkina, too, said these words, but with the whole story missing, her own meaning was dead. This important layer of the play was naturally incomprehensible and inevitably lost.

The second story is that of a barren fig tree in Lady's father's garden which miraculously bore fruit and which Lady decorated with Christmas ornaments as a symbol of re-birth. This story is a kind of apocryphal conclusion to the New Testament parable of the fig tree. Like this tree, Lady is first gifted with a second chance for fertility, then cursed with total and everlasting sterility. On the Moscow stage Lady did not tell the biblical story. It would have had no meaning either for her or for the audience. She danced her wonderful tarantella-triumph. The story implied the loss of illusion, but, according to the director's conception, she had to win even in death. "She wins," wrote the theatre critic Komissarzhevsky in his review of this production in the newspaper Sovetskaya Kultura (Soviet Culture). "Another Eurydice will go on the path of the "fugitive kind."[38] In the optimistic ending of the TTSA <u>Orpheus</u>, Carol proudly carried Val's snakeskin jacket, and she was followed approvingly by the projector's spotlight.

The artist is to be judged only according to the laws he himself has determined, believed Alexander Pushkin. Paraphrasing the words of the great Russian poet, we can say that the playwright is to be staged following his own rules, the inner laws of his poetics. In the ideologically controlled theatre it is rarely possible. On the Moscow stage, Williams's <u>Orpheus</u> turned into psychological drama with one heroine taking vengeance for her broken life. Kasatkina's highly professional and talented acting provided its own meaning, progression, and outcome. However, in this kind of interpretation, the image of Lady suffered from the loss of the theme of love and passion. For a better understanding of the sanctimonious treatment of Williams, we turn to the MXAT version of <u>Sweet Bird</u> (director V. Shilovsky) that also happened to be a drama staged for one actress.

Interrupting the dialogue of Chance and Scudder with a piercing shriek, Princess Kosmonopolis literally burst on to the stage. She did it convulsively and swiftly--like a wounded bird. She burst into and filled up the scenic space with the pleading and passionate, suffering and cruel modulations of her tremendous voice. This voice, a little hoarse but powerful and profound, was the unique and unforgetable voice of Angelina Stepanova.

A brilliant actress of the old Russian theatre, a student of the MXAT founders Stanislavsky and Nemirovich-Danchenko, Stepanova had been playing on the MXAT stage since 1924, when she came from the Third MXAT Studio. The Moscow Artistic Academic Theatre was considered by the Party in the thirties to be the one and only ideal of a true theatre, the artistic pattern which all other Soviet theatres had to follow. Stanislavsky's System was turned for years into a dogma of socialist realism. Angelina Stepanova, being a talented and unique artist, inevitably carried the seal of MXAT traditions in both the good and the bad meaning of this word. One of the last MXAT "Mohicans," Stepanova gained power over the theatre and became a kind of unofficial "Queen-Mother" to it. In 1975 she was not even able to say about herself, as Alexandra Del Lago did, "I am not old, I am just not young, not young." However, the theatre's Artistic Director, Oleg Efremov, and the producer of Sweet Bird, V. Shilovsky, had no choice but to give the famous actress the major part in Williams's play.

Stepanova was not afraid of looking old: the drama she played was one of an old, great actress who had outlived her own legend. Sharp movements of the fragile body in a winged blue tunic underlined her ailments; the shining blue silk mercilessly revealed an irreversible wasting away; and the fixed stare of terror-stricken eyes in an emaciated face told openly of the tormented soul of this woman. Princess-Stepanova choked with her shriek, shuddered with despair: "I have ... air ... shortage!!!" transmitting the sense of the stuffy air to the audience. Transitions of Princess-Stepanova from depression to excitement, from infantile capriciousness to impudent imperiousness, from delicate irony to rough cynicism--were swift and subtle. Stepanova's heroine did it naturally and without constraint, with the innate grace of a talented artist. Gradually, Chance's thinly concealed irritation disappeared, and he admitted with a smile: "I like you. You're a nice monster."[39]

Some Soviet critics thought of this Williams's character, with her desultory, almost incoherent words in the first scene, her senseless fits of anger and suspiciousness, as a Hollywood star who had gone crazy. The Soviet stereotype of Hollywood life was that of endless intrigues, fame, drugs, and numerous marriages. In his "Preface" to the book of Williams's plays (where Sweet Bird was not included!), V. Nedelin, a very serious and talented critic, wrote about Princess: "Her hysterical self-destruction and self-indulgence have gone so far that now she even exists in a kind of trance."[40]

However, Shilovsky and Stepanova did not agree with this interpretation. Yes, this Princess affirmed that she did not remember what Chance looked like, asked to repeat what failure had just been mentioned, did not know whether she wore glasses and so on. But just a few moments before, Alexandra Del Lago had pronounced, slowly and ponderably, as if it were an invocation: "I want to forget everything. I want to forget who I am." And, a second later, imperatively: "Please shut up, I am forgetting!"[41]

What Stepanova played was not the loss of memory,

but the intention to forget, to hypnotize herself into oblivion, and by that means finally to get some rest-- momentary, but a rest. She needed to rest her painful heart, to lessen the tension fettering her brain. Her nerves were shattered; the failure was tragic. But in these hard days had she lost her ability to sense beauty ("The birds cry so sadly ... ") or to speak ironically of herself ("I'll be the first lady in the Beanstalk country")?

The director's use of the proscenium was very interesting. Here, the function of the "fourth wall" was carried out by the imaginary windows opening on to a palm garden, and then " ... a strip of beach with some bathers and then, an infinite stretch of nothing but water."[42] That was the landscape described by Alexandra Del Lago. Chance would specify later: "The Gulf of misunderstanding."[43] Right here, by the imaginary windows overlooking this "Gulf of misunderstanding," Shilovsky created a "circle of truth," the entry into which led the characters to give up their lies and artificiality. The sorrowful theme of futile hopes and unrealized ideals of youth appeared in this "circle" in the monologues of Princess and Chance.

"There is nowhere to retire to when you retire from an art ... So, I retired to the moon, but the atmosphere of the moon does not have any oxygen in it. I began to feel breathless ... "[44] In Stepanova's performance, these thoughts coming out of the bottom of her own soul, expressed the thoughts of Alexandra Del Lago. She had everything: fame, wealth, admirers ... But the years had gone and the aged actress had decided to give up her art. At the same moment, the blooming earth had turned into a dead, withered planet. Money appeared as nothing but dust, and life depreciated. "Why the unsatisfied tiger? In the nerves jungle? Why is anything, anywhere, unsatisfied, and raging? ... I could not get old with that tiger still in me raging ... "[45] Stepanova was faithful to Williams with all her heart and soul, believing in her lines: "You can't retire with the outcrying heart of an artist still crying out in your body, in your nerves ... "[45] This phrase was translated specially for Stepanova: "You can't leave the stage when the soul of an actress is still crying out ... " So, Alexandra Del Lago was forced to be more forgetful than she intended and to speak of herself as an actress of the stage, not of the movies.

Princess left the "circle of truth," hastily dried her eyes, and again buttoned herself up in an impenetrable shell of cantankerousness, suspiciousness, and irony. She did it right in time, for Chance (actor I. Vasiliev), occupied much more with his own plans than with the old actress' torments, was desperately attempting to exploit her fame and connections. No shade of fear clouded the face of Stepanova's character when she said: "I hate to think of what kind of desperation has made you try to intimidate me. ME? ALEXANDRA DEL LAGO? It's so silly, it's touching, downright endearing,"[46] she exclaimed. Right away she dictated her own demands which were humiliating for Chance.

In the script, Williams says clearly and repeatedly what kind of paid services Chance has to perform. The translators (Vulf and Doroshevich) and the MXAT "softened" the text "a little" and "slightly veiled the motives,"[47] as it was phrased in the review of this production in the Teatr magazine.

After a "little" softening and as a result of "slightly veiled" motives, the meaning of Sweet Bird as a play and "sweet bird" as Williams's symbol were inevitably changed. The theme of sexuality as a liberating and, at the same time, a destructive force that pervades all of Williams's writing, had disappeared. This theme was unacceptable to Party officials, who checked all productions before their premieres, and to the aged actress for whom the mention of love-making was not only immoral but grotesque. (Princess, of course, despised decency and morality!) On the Moscow stage, Williams was forced to be "decent." His play had been smoothed and straightened. The MXAT, the "ideal" Soviet theatre, did not like the idea of having the "monstrous" side of human nature shown on its renowned stage.

Princess-Stepanova did speak of herself and Chance as monsters. "We are two monsters, but with this difference between us. Out of the passion and torment of my existence I have created a thing that I can unveil, a sculpture almost heroic ... which is true."[48] "Which is art," said Stepanova correcting Williams. And then, trying to clarify his symbols she added a phrase he never wrote: "The sweet bird of youth that sings in my soul is the craving for creation!" "In these words," Marina Smelyanskaya wrote in the review cited above, "there are her happiness in participation in art, pride for her talent, and a hymn to the sweet bird of youth. The MXAT saw in Williams's symbolic image of a sweet bird the incarnation of everything beautiful that exists in the human soul: talent, selflessness, nobility--all that is so peculiar to youth and that people so often lose in life's struggles."49

But whose selflessness and nobility did the critic and the company see in this play? Chance's? Alexandra Del Lago's? The final long monologue of Princess was interpreted as her "starry hour," the highest point of her spiritual development. At this moment, her influence on Chance was so strong that even he became serious and restrained as if he were rising above himself and his good-for-nothing life. He made his choice and persuading him to leave was useless; so great was the power of art and a real artist.

However, in Williams's paradoxical view on art, an artist, unique and creative, could somehow become a destructive force both for himself and for those close to him. Princess, in some respects, becomes a witness and accessory to Chance's destruction. She is in a way, his "angel of death." Her instinct for survival enables her to abandon him. (As Val is an "angel of death" for Lady and Carol, or Tom Wingfield--for his mother and sister). Princess teaches Chance to accept his mutilation as, indeed, she leads him to self-recognition. "What else can you be?" she asks. Chance replies: "Nothing ... But not part of your luggage."50 In this respect, Williams makes his aged actress into the Lady of the Lake (Del Lago) who gives Chance his sword of self-recognition with one hand and takes the sword away with the other when she leaves him to be castrated.

MXAT performing and stylistic traditions rooted in realistic theatre, turned out to be not quite suitable for such philosophical and dramatic paradoxes as those of Williams. The complex and conflicting portrait of a great actress who can flee from a fiasco into a familiar, sordid round of sex, drugs, and drink--turned out to be unacceptable for the image that the leading MXAT actress wanted to portray.

Brilliantly, in the best Stanislavsky's tradition, Stepanova made us understand what was going on in the soul of her heroine. After her pathetic confession about the meaning and power of art, Princess suddenly lapsed into silence. She was totally exhausted and enveloped by weariness and terror. We saw that her future was not so rosy as it had seemed only a moment before. Again, Chance and Princess were led by the director into the "circle of truth": they sat side-by-side on the suitcases like passengers who had missed their station or like homeless children lost in the "Beanstalk Country." "I am dead as old Egypt," said Princess-Stepanova. Then she rose tiredly, gently touched Chance's shoulder, and for the last time offered him help and rescue, which he irrevocably refused. Silently and wearily, Alexandra Del Lago left the stage as an old star who had outlived her own legend.

On the Moscow stage, Chance did not come forward to make his curtain speech to the audience asking for understanding and compassion or at least recognition. At the very end of his play, Williams tells us through Chance that his drama is about our major enemy--time--and what time does to us all. However, in the MXAT, Williams's play turned into a psychological drama about a great and old actress, sometimes desperately embittered but mostly majestic and understanding. In the best tradition of the Russian psychological theatre, she told about her torments. Indeed, in <u>Sweet Bird</u>, Williams does pay tribute to the many heroic, aging actresses he had watched master his roles and their own lives simultaneously: Laurette Taylor, Helen Hayes, Tallulah Bankhead, Diana Barrymore ... His Princess is no simple archetype. She incorporates the complexity and ambiguity of individuals Williams had come to know and admire in his long theatre-life. But although loving and admiring, he, at the same time, saw the "monstrous" part of his characters' souls. Alexandra Del Lago is not only a great actress and an embodiment of the power of art. Recognizing time as the ultimate enemy for both Chance and herself, she can acknowledge that they were both monsters living in the Beanstalk Country. Why does she pity Chance? Because of her big heart and selflessness, as portrayed on the MXAT stage?--Or is it because Chance, an inadequate monster, having neither talent nor character, has wasted his store of good looks and good will so quickly and so foolishly?

When Princess mentions the castration to which Chance is doomed, he replies: "You did that to me this morning, here on this bed."[51] She in turn acknowledges her own impotence: "Age does the same thing to a woman." "Both are faced with castration,"[51] as Williams indicates. But as we have seen, the epilogue of the Moscow version was absolutely different from the script. Not only the theme of castration but even the word itself was removed from the text. For Williams, castration (or rape, as in <u>Streetcar</u>) is an effective image for what time and society do to the majority of us and to the most sensitive--the artists--first. Blanche is raped; in <u>Orpheus</u>, the characters toy with the idea of castration; in <u>Sweet Bird</u>, they carry out their threat. Time robs the artist of his dreams (a sweet bird of youth--talent, love, passion--is castrated), and then the world uses the artist for its own diversion. <u>Sweet Bird</u> tells us not only of a great old actress and a love affair broken up by a malicious political leader. Here we have a man who is to be castrated, a woman who has had a hysterectomy, a man who is impotent or nearly so, and another woman for whom love means sex which is no more than a temporary release from panic, like hashish or pill. Does all that concern only the power of art as the MXAT suggested? There is also the power of mindless violence, coercion, and the crassest use of money to gain degraded or evil ends. These things cannot be omitted from the play: the character of Alexandra Del Lago is indeed like the soul of art--suffering, devouring, enduring, perhaps even triumphant. But Williams also shows us how culture and art can be dissipated through fear and misuse, and how an artist can collapse into drugs and sexual degradation. In the Soviet "corrected," "smoothed," and "straightened" version of his play, Williams himself had to go through what he had always expected and feared: spiritual and ideological castration.

We have seen the kinds of transformations Williams's heroines, Lady and Princess, underwent on the Moscow stage. Now we will turn to the images of his Orpheus-like saviors, Val and Chance, and see how they were handled.

In the TTSA, Val was played by A. Vasiliev. If Kasatkina, with her strict and restrained acting manner had an inclination to tragedy, Vasiliev played as if in a drama of everyday life. He found a natural, unexpressive intonation that remained unchanged throughout the whole performance and never went beneath the surface. Vasiliev depicted a man who was at home everywhere. He appeared a little bit impudent because of his spontaneous frankness, but in fact, he was really indifferent to everything, tired and apathetic. Williams thought of his play as a "tale of a wild-spirited boy who wanders into a conventional community of the South and creates the commotion of a fox in a chicken coop."[52] How could the inhabitants of Two River County be infuriated by Val as he was portrayed on the TTSA stage?

The author's cherished thoughts (like the famous line "we're all of us locked up tight inside our own bodies")[53] were spoken by Val-Vasiliev as if they were somebody else's words, prepared in advance, without emotion. His feelings for Lady were also unconvincing. It seemed that this Val was taking her love only for his own comfort and convenience. Even at the moment when he learned about Lady's pregnancy, his reaction looked forced and unnatural. In this interpretation, the tragic destiny of Williams's hero became not more than meaningless bad luck connected only with the outward plot. Whether this interpretation was intentional one could not easily judge for lack of "ensemble." There was a certain artistic disorder in this production. Spectacular effects and outward characterization were not infrequently substituted for precision of interpretation. The major reason for it was probably the diffusion of the producer's artistic intention.

Actually in this play, Williams gives an image of a mythical Orpheus that is far from conventional. If we consider Williams to be among the Orphic writers, he is surely the one with the most extraordinary and paradoxical attitude toward this theme. For him, Orpheus is not just an image that can suggest the supernatural power of art and artist. His Orphic characters always carry hell inside themselves. The playwright's idea of Orpheus has something to do with a strong sense of damnation, with a touch of poetry in a human being who cannot bear life, rather than with the traditional image of an artist-savior. His "Orpheus Descending" is not looking for a Eurydice although hell is full of them. He has come to Hades because this is his thirtieth birthday: it is time to settle down and live like everybody else. The motif of Orpheus' unsuccessful capitulation was one of the most important in the play.

The TTSA Val also came to Two River County penitentially. "I am looking for a job," he explained. "I'm done with the life that I've been leading ... I'm not young any more."[54] But this Val, who looked like a fellow from some working class suburb of a big city, seemed to come out of a typical Soviet play about ideal workers and socialist competition. The key in which Vasiliev played his role would have been suitable for a play about everyday life but it did not work in Williams's mythological drama. Of course, Val is neither a subtle dreamer nor a heroic-looking rebel. But he certainly is not a character out of a propagandist play. He has to be a man who cannot get accustomed to the world everybody else lives in. (That was the way the majority of Soviet readers understood Williams's hero. I even happened to come across the point of view of Val as a type in some respects similar to Alexander Ginzburg--perhaps that Ginzburg as he was at the time when he thought himself separated from the regime by means of his purely poetical "samizdat" magazine, <u>Syntax</u>.) Of course there are no specific connections between Williams's play and Soviet dissidents, but people very often see what they are looking for in a work of art.

Orpheus' illusion is that he can settle down and accommodate to the world and still remain Orpheus: to be free from hell while remaining in hell. However, half-way capitulation does not suit hell. Society has never trusted Orpheus. This idea is very important. Probably it was originally important for the TTSA (perhaps that was why Val was done as an ordinary, everyday-looking guy), but it failed to transmit this concept to the audience.

In the TTSA approach to the image of Val, his symbolic "birth" from the old man's Choctaw cry was absolutely unmotivated. According to the script, Val appears when all the elements of the tragedy are ready, and at Carol's request, mysterious Uncle Pleasant gives his animalistic cry that sounds like a desperate appeal for help. Who is this old sorcerer smiling out of the darkness? What kind of connection exists between Williams's modern Orpheus and this ancient savage cry? Does the Conjure man's cry suggest Val's symbolic Dionysian link with the animal kingdom?

The acting edition of <u>Orpheus</u> is prefaced by Williams with Strindberg's note to Paul Gauguin in which he speaks of "an immense need to become a savage and create a new world." This particular edition was translated into Russian with Strindberg's words as an epigraph. "Something is still wild in this country," says Carol. Probably only a fugitive kind, unruly and wild, the author wants to say, can spiritually resist hell. Williams's symbols are never easy to express and realize on the stage. However, Burdonsky, as director, should have somehow tried to understand the Conjure man and his link with Val. Just the formal obedience to the playwright's remarks did not work at all. Uncle Pleasant remained an alien and obscure figure in this production.

There was an analogous lack of understanding of Val's Orphic dimensions as a savior. Of course, any religious allusions to his name that suggested the Christian martyr and salvation (Valentine and Xavier-savior) were not generally noticed by the Soviet public. Even if they were recognized, those allusions would not have been acceptable on a stage that was considered to be one of the main ideological fronts. For Williams, however, the divine nature of his hero, whose destruction takes place on "the Saturday before Easter," was very important. His Val descends into death's underworld and remains there; no resurrection occurs. Before Williams, the Orphic myth had been too optimistic. In Williams's interpretation, it reached the point of no return.

Perhaps even a Western or American audience of <u>Orpheus</u> would have been more sensitive to the cruelty of the little town toward the wanderer-musician than to the mythological or Christian allusions. However, the omission of the concept of Val as a messianic hero who was always expected by the sufferers of Two River County (as occurred at the TTSA), was a mortal wound to the play itself.

One might say that there was no way for the Soviet theatre to stage a play with even a shade of religious allusion. However, other approaches were possible. The complicated and conflicting image of Val as a messianic, doomed, and destructive savior could be rooted in his artistic nature as well as in his divine origin. There was an attempt to do it at the TTSA. Val-Vasiliev had a guitar which he claimed to be his "life-companion." He sang the ballad "Heavenly Grass," and even tried to convince the audience of the important (if not mythic and ritualistic) meaning of his music. "It washes me clean like water, when anything unclean touched me."[55]

However, one important aspect was overlooked. Val is not only an artist in the literary or musical sense. For Williams, it is also necessary that he be an artist-philosopher seeking an ultimate answer. Williams suggested that his play was about two kinds of people, those who accepted the "prescribed answers that were not answers at all," and those described in a key phrase of the play as "fugitive kind," who continued to ask "the unanswered questions that haunt the heart of people."56

Probably in a situation where ideological check-ups were inevitable, Burdonsky, as director, did not want to risk the whole production by portraying the boy who sought the ultimate truth of the world he lived in.

So, as we have seen, there were subjective and objective reasons for the failure of the Soviet portrayal of Val. A confused artistic conception, along with poor casting, may be considered as subjective; the impossibility of including religious and sexual references may be thought of as objective. Sexual and sensual feelings pervade Williams's writing. His Orpheus-like heroes are usually described as "good-looking" or "very good-looking" and they are gifted with a highly-charged sexual magnetism. The TTSA changed the starting point, and the actor tried to explain Val's incredible charm by means of his music, whereas it should have resided more in his inherent sexuality. In Williams, those who are in hell consider sexual salvation one of the ways out. Blanche uses the "intimacies with strangers" as attempts to escape the horror of her soul. Carol Cutrere thinks sexual love is the only way to feel, even through pain, that "you are alive." We have seen how in the Mayakovsky Theatre, Blanche was turned into an almost sexless image of light in the world of darkness. In the TTSA, Carol did not give the lines about love-making and her "jookings." They were simply cut out of the text. These kinds of omissions were detrimental to the meaning of Williams's plays. In the case of Chance Wayne in <u>Sweet Bird</u>, they happened to be even more crucial than they were in the case with the TTSA <u>Orpheus</u>.

On the MXAT stage, a very attractive young man paced the floor of a comfortable hotel room. However, the luxurious surroundings obviously did not give him peace of mind. There were only a few moments when Chance Wayne was alone on stage; the audience needed to use this occasion to examine him as an individual. In the presence of others, Chance (played coincidently by I. Vasiliev) would be continuously changing his masks, adapting to the person with whom he talked. When the first moment of solitude was interrupted by the entrance of a black waiter (artist Z. Tobolsev), we witnessed the first of Chance's transformations. He put on a mask of a haughty millionaire. However, his unexplained irritability and nervous movements revealed Chance's inner turmoil. Later, he would try on various conflicting roles: a lady-killer who was also in love with himself; a failure, touching in his helplessness; a calculating blackmailer; an idealist absorbed in the ideas of his youth. However, Vasiliev's character was not a very skillful actor. Therefore we perceived Chance as if he were two-dimensional: on the one hand, there was his pretended spiritual condition; on the other--his real feelings that he was unable to conceal. Not only did these conditions lack convergence but they were almost diametrically opposite; and Vasiliev, as an actor, could not always succeed in solving this complicated dilemma.

The actor's best moments were in the episode with George Scudder (actor V. Stepanov), when Chance's bombastic bravado invariably contasted with Scudder's sober rationalism. "Your mother is dead. A couple of weeks ago." Bare facts were lashing Chance. His self-satisfied smile hardened and became preposterous and pitiful. His hands started fussing mechanically, moving pillows on the sofa. He asked two or three meaningless questions, and then again attempted to conceal himself behind the mask of well-being. Scudder's next attack was more painful. "I wrote you that a certain girl we know had to go through an awful experience, a tragic ordeal, because of past contact with you." Chance's affected pose of deliberate respectability, his velvety intonations disappeared and were forgotten. "What ordeal? What girl? Heavenly? Heavenly? Heavenly?"[57] Chance-Vasiliev screamed out again and again.

However, in general, Vasiliev did not see in his role anything worthy of compassion or understanding. His Chance had no psychological riddles. His personality was all spread out before our eyes: an ignorant and light-headed fellow. There was nothing but silly boasting in Chance's words when Vasiliev said: "I had some kind of quantity "X" in my blood, a wish or a need to be different ... "[58] Even inside the "circle of truth," Vasiliev affected a variety of poses and gave his voice a preposterous pomposity.

The actor interpreted Chance's worship of beauty (his love for Heavenly) as mere self-admiration--a desire to demonstrate to himself that he was no longer a vicious child but a virtuous adult. Heartlessness, narrow-mindness, conceit and indifference to anything but immediate pleasure--these were the traits Vasiliev saw in his character. The attitude of both actor and director toward Chance was absolutely merciless. They made him appear a mere pretender, both silly and cruel, leading the life of a good-for-nothing.

Of course this Williams's character is a marginal artist at best, or perhaps simply a failure. (As Val is an unfulfilled artist: in <u>Battle of Angels</u>, he does not finish his book; in <u>Orpheus</u>, he gives up his career as a musician). Chance, as an actor, assumes, or at least tries to assume various roles throuhout the play--son, blackmailer, lover. He plays a romantic with Aunt Nannie, a sophisticate with the waiter and barman, and finally a fatalist, appealing to the audience for understanding. We remember that in a high school drama competition, Chance had forgotten his lines. He has never been a competent actor. However, he is not that silly and narrow-minded, unsympathetic character who appeared on the Moscow stage.

For Williams, it was very important that Chance had some qualities of the artist. Chance, like Val, reaches for the sky--for Heavenly, for St. Cloud, for Kosmonopolis, for Hollywood. The necessity of this idea to the image of Chance and to the play itself, was not understood in the MXAT, which was the reason the interpretation appeared one-sided and impoverished; Chance was merely a temporary partner of a great actress. In the producer's conception, there was no thought of Chance being important by and for himself: as an artist, as an everlasting stranger, as an alien element in the society, and therefore, as a man doomed.

This one-sided approach to the role of Chance led to the loss of other aspects of Williams's concept of the artist and of the sense of damnation fundamental to his plays. Williams's artistic characters are invariably associated with destruction, either their own or that of someone close. Because of some weakness or predisposition, they unconsciously court their own disasters (for example, Val's decision to stay ensures his own destruction). Chance also exhibits self-destructive tendencies which involve acceptance of castration. In the MXAT production, however, Chance suddenly changed after having been influenced by Alexandra Del Lago's talent and personality as a great actress. After her monologue of a sweet bird of youth and art, he made his choice. Vasiliev exhibited dignity in his reconciliation with inevitable death. Shilovsky, as director, saw no other explanation for Chance's decision to stay and pay for his guilt.

Stanislavsky taught, when playing a malicious character, try to find his good sides. However, for the traditional Russian psychological acting style, the self-destructive tendencies of Williams's Orpheus-like characters were incomprehensible as abnormal and impossible to portray realistically. It seemed easier and more routine to find an explanation in the world outside the character. Here the director rationalized that it was the old actress who forced the young man to feel the suffering he caused and to bear the burden of his guilt.

But inextricably involved in this play are Christian and mythological symbolism: the action takes place on Easter Sunday, and each of the main characters hopes for rebirth. As in the TTSA <u>Orpheus</u>, this symbolism was destined for omission. Perhaps one can say that religious allusions do not play so important a role in <u>Sweet Bird</u> as they do in <u>Orpheus</u>. But Williams's treatment of the theme of the Crucifixion can be related, in some respects, to that of Faulkner in <u>Light in August</u> (Both Joe Christmas and Chance are castrated). This novel was translated into Russian almost at the time of <u>Sweet Bird</u>'s premiere. If, in Faulkner's case, the parallel worked, in Williams's case it probably did not. His hero, Chance Wayne, guilty of real sexual misconduct and other evils, seeing no possibility of living, is ready to sacrifice himself to avoid hurting himself and others. However, the script does not make clear whether it is real sacrifice, masochism, self-deception, or perhaps the most unchristian of emotions--despair. It is up to the director to find his own interpretation for what takes place on that Easter Sunday in St. Cloud. Of course, no Easter Sunday was possible on the MXAT stage, but Shilovsky and Vasiliev, as we have seen, gave Chance a degree of self-recognition under the influence of the famous actress. Unfortunately that looked too simple and unconvincing.

But the elimination of the sexual aspect of Chance's character proved to be even more detrimental to the play than the removal of the religious issue.

To Williams, Chance represented love and passion. His yearning for Heavenly, his ability to give love, his illusion of perpetual youth were all very important for the author. In the interpretation of Vasiliev, however, Chance appeared insincere in regard to Heavenly; his story of youthful love came across as merely a hymn to a sweet bird of youth. Chance, as portrayed by Vasiliev, seemed incapable of the one talent the playwright gave him--the talent for love.

There is a paradoxical view of sexuality in Williams's plays. Sexual love is the opposite of death; it represents a drive to live, and sex is a repeated metaphor for an ecstatic life lived fully in the present moment. In Sweet Bird of Youth, Chance expresses the view: "The great difference between people in this world is not between the rich and the poor, or the good and the evil, but between the ones that have pleasure in love and those who haven't."[59] Sexuality is transformed into salvation when it seems to be life's only fulfillment. Then it becomes an attempt to find God in one's fellow-man in a world which God Himself seems to have forsaken. It was probably characteristic for the Soviet ideological attitude toward sexual love and the religious meaning of salvation that in the MXAT, Chance did not say these words to Princess, nor was there a character in the crowd who uttered the truth about total silence and speechlessness of God in our world.

But for Williams, there was another side to passion: it could maim and kill, often in the most violent fashion. Probably there are some connections between these fates: Blanche is raped and driven insane; Val is burnt to death; Chance Wayne is castrated--all as a result of sexual drives. The only salvation from loneliness--human sexuality--is revealed as man's original sin. Yet, Sweet Bird is not as pessimistic as one might conclude (although the seeming pessimism and also the violence of this play were the major reasons why on the MXAT stage it was turned into the story of a famous old actress). The author wants us to see that without love and compassion, life is meaningless, despite the fact that possession of these qualities may lead a person to destruction. With them, life can be tolerated, if not completely enjoyed. Williams's artists--saviors, victims, destroyers--recognize that fact. However, as throughout history, the artists in Williams are prophets without honor in their own land, Dragon or Beanstalk Country, and they are usually destroyed.

By confessing his sins and accepting his death, Chance Wayne has gotten absolution--a superior innocence after the fall. Likewise Val, in the fire of a blowtorch finally achieves the desired purification from the corrupting earth, becoming eternally a fugitive kind. Perhaps Williams wanted to prove with the deaths of his heroes that time and society do not triumph after all. But on the Moscow stage, the deaths of Chance Wayne and Val Xavier were not motivated by the author's inmost ideas. These characters were moved to the background of the productions and reduced to the roles of simple partners for the main heroines. Dramatically deprived of their major meanings, Williams's artists had to undergo second deaths, for which neither they nor Williams were to blame.

NOTES

35 Tennessee Williams, "Foreword" to <u>Sweet Bird of Youth</u>, p. 647.

36 Tennessee Williams, <u>Orpheus Descending</u>, p. 551.

37 Tennessee Williams, <u>Orpheus Descending</u>, p. 601.

38 V. Komissarzhevsky, "Lestnitsa na Kryshu: Pesy Tennessi Uilyamsa na Sovetskoy Stsene," <u>Sovetskaya Kultura</u>, 28 Fevr. 1978. (V. Kommissarzhevsky, "Stairs to the Roof: Tennessee Williams's Plays on the Soviet Stage," <u>Soviet Culture</u>, 28 Febr. 1978).

39 Tennessee Williams, <u>Sweet Bird of Youth</u>, p. 662.

40 V. Nedelin, "Doroga Zhizni v Pesakh Tennessi Uilyamsa," v <u>Steklyanny Zverinets i Eshche Devyat Pes</u>, str. 717. (V. Nedelin, "The Road of Life in Tennessee Williams's Dramas," in <u>The Glass Menagerie and Nine Other Plays</u>, p. 717).

41 Tennessee Williams, <u>Sweet Bird of Youth</u>, p. 660.

42 Tennessee Williams, <u>Sweet Bird of Youth</u>, p. 668.

43 Tennessee Williams, <u>Sweet Bird of Youth</u>, p. 670.

44 Tennessee Williams, <u>Sweet Bird of Youth</u>, p. 668.

45 Tennessee Williams, <u>Sweet Bird of Youth</u>, p. 669.

46 Tennessee Williams, <u>Sweet Bird of Youth</u>, p. 675.

47 M. Smelyanskaya, "Preodolet Sebya: <u>Sladkogolosaya Ptitsa Yunosti</u> Tennessi Uilyamsa vo M.Kh.A.Te," <u>Teatr</u>, No. 6 (1977), str. 21. (M. Smelyanskaya, "To Overcome Yourself: Tennessee Willimas's <u>Sweet Bird of Youth</u> in the MXAT," <u>Theatre</u>, p. 21).

48 Tennessee Williams, <u>Sweet Bird of Youth</u>, p. 732.

49 M. Smelyanskaya, "Preodolet Sebya," str. 21.

50 Tennessee Williams, *Sweet Bird of Youth*, p. 733.

51 Tennessee Williams, *Sweet Bird of Youth*, p. 732.

52 Tennessee Williams, "The Past, the Present, and the Perhaps," p. 540.

53 Tennessee Williams, *Orpheus Descending*, p. 583.

54 Tennessee Williams, *Orpheus Descending*, p. 562.

55 Tennessee Williams, *Orpheus Descending*, p. 574.

56 Tennessee Williams, "The Past, the Present, and the Perhaps," p. 540.

57 Tennessee Williams, *Sweet Bird of Youth*, p. 657.

58 Tennessee Williams, *Sweet Bird of Youth*, p. 678.

59 Tennessee Williams, *Sweet Bird of Youth*, p. 681.

CHAPTER V

STRUGGLE FOR PROPERTY OR WORLD BEFORE THE FLOOD:

KINGDOM OF EARTH IN MOSCOW AND LENINGRAD

In December, 1977, when Moscow was snow-covered, Williams's "Flood" threatened the mercenary and self-interested "kingdom of earth" created on the stage of the Moscow Mossoviet Theatre (Teatr imeni Mossoveta). A few months later, in 1978, Myrtle's descents had begun in the Leningrad Theatre of Drama and Comedy on Liteiny Prospekt. The "funny melodrama,"[60] as Williams referred to Kingdom of Earth in his Memoirs, appeared on the stages of both Russian capitals almost simultaneously. It might have been chance; but perhaps by the end of the seventies, the Soviet theatre was beginning to sense the necessity of revealing the destructive influence of modern life on human personality, and to realize the need to find forces capable of withstanding this destruction. In any case, in the winter of 1978, both in Leningrad and in Moscow, Williams's play appeared to be in tune with the time.

The ideas and images of this play had been present in Williams's imagination for almost twenty years. First produced in 1968 as Seven Descents of Myrtle, it derived from "The Kingdom of Earth," a short story published in 1954 and included in The Knightly Quest and Other Stories (1966). Williams turned the story into many different theatrical versions: first, a one-act play; then a longer play produced in Florida; another variant staged in Spoleto; one written for Esquire; a Broadway revision; and finally, in 1975, a new variation. This was a remarkable effort even for a dramatist known for his revisions.

The Seven Descents of Myrtle opened in an off-Broadway theatre on March 27, 1968, and closed after twenty-nine performances, on April 20. In 1970, Sidney Lumet made the play into a film called Last of the Mobile Hot Shots, which was also unsuccessful. However, in spite of all these failures, Williams came back to the play and created a new version, using the title of the original story, Kingdom of Earth. What was it in this story that had captured the playwright's imagination for almost twenty years?

The story begins on a night when the raging Mississippi threatens to submerge Two River County.

67

Despite the threat, a young man named Lot, returns to the farm he has inherited from his mother, Miss Lottie. The farm is being run by Lot's half-brother, dark-complexioned Chicken, to whom Lot had willed the property in a signed agreement. Now, although dying of tuberculosis, weak and moribund, Lot brings home a new bride--buxom, loud-voiced Myrtle, a vaudeville actress whom he has married on television. Lot impresses Myrtle with golden chairs and a crystal chandelier, the choice of his mother, who worshipped beauty and elegance. In contrast, he describes with disgust the crudeness of his father and his fatner's son, Chicken. His hope is that this marriage to Myrtle will invalidate the agreement he had signed with Chicken. The scenes alternate between the kitchen, which is Chicken's world, associated with food and sex, and the bedroom upstairs, where Lot sits silently wearing his "Mona Lisa" smile. This bedroom, along with the elegant parlor below, has become a kind of mausoleum for the beautiful dead Miss Lottie; it has now also become Lot's world. Myrtle is manipulated by both men in their struggle against one another. Lot orders her to steal from Chicken the signed agreement--the paper with which he never parts. In order to gain Chicken's trust, Myrtle attempts to win his friendship. Soon she is ordered by him to steal the marriage license from Lot. The contrast between the brothers becomes increasingly a caricature. Dressed in his mother's silk robe, smoking a cigarette in an ivory holder, Lot instructs Myrtle to hit Chicken on the head if she cannot get the agreement in any other way. Instead, infuriated by Lot, who has called her a "whore," she obeys Chicken and grabs the marriage license. Taken at surface level alone, the play is indeed a funny melodrama, both difficult and strange.

The earthy Chicken triumphs over his effete half-brother by seducing Myrtle, promising to rescue her life in a flood and offering her some chance of a future more satisfying than her unfortunate past. Chicken proclaims his "philosophy" that "what is happening between a man and a woman," a "perfick understandin," as Myrtle puts it, is the most important thing in the world. All the rest, Chicken believes, is "crap."61 The stage business revolves around phenomena that are both natural and symbolic--the weather, hurricane and flood, and the need to ascend to the roof, where Myrtle hopes to be saved. (We may recall here Williams's <u>Baby Doll</u> and the Meighan attic, where Baby Doll's sense of life is heightened).

If we look closer at the material which underlies the "funny" surface, Kingdom of Earth may be revealed additionally as a work of great power and compelling intensity. For Estelle Parsons, who played Myrtle in the Broadway production, what was central to the play was "the exploration of the characters more than a story line."62 However, perhaps the importance of Kingdom of Earth lies in both characters and story line. This three-character "rabelaisian comedy," as Williams called it, is also reminiscent of Blanche Du Bois' tragic encounter with Stanley and Stella. Here too in a conflict between the delicate, elegant character and his crude, healthy opponents, it is the combined power of the opponents that wins out. Indeed, it seems that in Kingdom of Earth as in Streetcar, those who survive are the strong and brutal.

Chicken, like Stanley, even eats raw meat (chicken's blood), but there is more to Chicken than mere strength and brutality. The playwright spoke of him as "a lonesome, illegitimate half-breed who, finding the solace of religion inadequate, succumbs happily to the wisdom of the flesh."63 The personalities of Myrtle and Lot also reflect major changes in the playwright's points of view since the writing of his earlier plays. Lot, despite his refinement and quest for beauty, lacks the nobility of spirit which characterized the artist figures in Williams's earlier days, although in some respects he is like Blanche, or Val, or Sebastian--too sensitive to survive. Williams told Estelle Parsons that in killing Lot, he was "killing all the wispy, willowy women he had written about."64

Myrtle, is an artist figure (she used to be in show business), but she is an artist in the playwright's later mode. We may recall here Nonno, an artist from the Night of the Iguana who, like many of Williams's artists, dies in the play. But Nonno dies at the age of ninety-seven; obviously his grip on reality has been sufficient to account for this long survival.

Signi Falk in her book Tennessee Williams, cites the critics' opinions about the Kingdom of Earth. For example, Wilfred Sheed described the play as " ... traditional of neohomosexual theatre ... the steady, fly-wing pulling humiliation of a woman, whipsawed and put upon by a fag and a stud."65 Some critics, John Simon for example, were struck by the play as self-parroting and self-parody. Signi Falk herself was convinced that Kingdom of Earth "perhaps was written to make money," and described it as a "shabby piece." But it seems improbable to me that a mere "shabby piece" and the desire of self-parodying would have remained in the mind of such an artist as Tennessee Williams for almost twenty years. Perhaps something important in this play was overlooked by the critics.

It may be helpful to return to two major symbols which we know occupied Williams's imagination: the Flood and the Roof. The Roof allows an escape from the frighteningly empty, burning or flooded house. The Roof may also help one to get close to the sky and see Val's favorite blue birds of freedom that "sleep on the wind and never get to the ground."[66] The symbol of the roof may have many meanings to Williams and sometimes even comes into the titles of his plays, such as Stairs to the Roof or Cat on a Hot Tin Roof.

Roofs were still a preoccupation of Williams at the end of the sixties, the end of "The Stoned Age," (as he referred to the years of his total collapse in his Memoirs), when he returned to the three-character play. He did it for more than reasons of either money or self-parody. Although his Kingdom of Earth concerns hatred, love, self-interest and broken illusions, he wanted in this play to affirm understanding and love as the only way of salvation through the symbolic rising to the roof on the night of the flood. Soon after the Broadway version was written (1968), Williams became a Roman Catholic, although he did not accept the concept of immortality. The "kingdom of earth," despite the fact that it wallowed in vice, was still of major importance to him.

We are now ready to examine the Soviet interpretations of this play. The Moscow and Leningrad productions were totally different. The Moscow performance, directed by Pavel Khomsky, was accompanied by a program which included a brief article entitled "Tennessee Williams and His Play," written by Vulf, the translator. Probably the theatre feared that this drama, never published in Russian and totally unknown to the public, would be interpreted "wrong." This is how Kingdom of Earth was introduced to the Moscow theatre-goers:

> Williams's dramas are distin-
> guished by the author's desire to

expose social motives under the cover of psychological conflict. He is a major artist, who resists, perhaps unconsciously, the heartlessness and lack of spirituality which characterize American life. He attacks racism and cruelty, which are hateful to him, but he intuitively points out the healthy need for moral ideals.67

Just a few lines in Vulf's introduction were devoted to the play itself: "Kingdom of Earth is a play about brutality and kindness ... Nothing can stop Tennessee Williams in his search for goodness and humanity."67 Then again the public was directed how and where to see the meaning in the works of this American playwright. "Human tragedies that are performed on the wordly stage in Williams's dramas are nothing but the corollaries of social vices deep-rooted in American life. This is the social meaning of his dramas."67

On the Moscow stage, as we shall see, Williams's play was deliberately deprived of its symbolic ideas; the theme appeared to be merely the struggle for the farm and the mercenary motives of its three characters. However, we must remember that this was the very first production of Kingdom of Earth. Only a doctrinal approach could have made possible its presentation in Moscow. The situation in Leningrad, however, was a little easier. The drama itself had already been approved by the state capital and was successfully showing on the stage of one of its leading theatres. Kama Ginkas, in the Theatre of Drama and Comedy on Liteiny Prospekt, as we shall see, staged a very complex, serious and philosophical performance, that still may be regarded as one of the best Soviet productions of Williams. The difference in approach between the Moscow and Leningrad interpretations was somehow felt by the audiences from their first glances at the settings.

Ginkas interpreted Williams's play as an almost Biblical story of three people in a world that was about to be destroyed by the Flood, three human beings and each one a mystery. There were three actors whose mission it was to solve this mystery. With the help of Eduard Kochergin, who met the qualification of "very gifted designer," which Williams specified in his first stage directions to the play, Ginkas created the stage image that plunged us immediately into the strange atmosphere--a thrilling fusion of ruthlessness, perishing beauty, and ... tenderness.

There was a vertical section of the house. On the left, we could see a little parlor with the gilded chairs and crystal chandelier. Those things, beautiful once, in a time of refinement and elegance, now looked neglected and lonely. In the center, there was a dark hall with a flight of stairs to a bedroom which was dim when the curtain rose. A gloomy kitchen, stage-right, was starkly functional, with crude, unpainted table, stools and rigid bed. The designer and the director had in mind a favorite Williams's theme: the contrast between the world of a refined and dying aristocracy and a gross but productive plebian world. The velvet draperies and golden chairs--elegance and taste, grace and style--not only illustrated Miss Lottie's aristocratic pretensions but also served as ironic counterpoint to the sensual life of the kitchen, spirit opposed to body, as in the play <u>Summer</u> and <u>Smoke</u>.

The sound and light score were as important to this production as they were to Williams himself. In his "Production Notes" to <u>The Glass Menagerie</u> Williams wrote that "the transformation of truth, life and reality" was important, not for the sake of distortion, but to "find a closer approach to truth, a more penetrating and vivid expression of things as they are."[68] Ginkas and Kochergin shared this goal. For his <u>Kingdom of Earth</u>, Williams wanted "the mood of a blue song whose subject is loneliness" (Stage Directions to scene one). From the first moments of the Leningrad production we heard the low, menacing murmur of water and the moaning of wind. At the same time, a pipe's melody started (an innovation of the director). Wild and harrowing, played by the yet invisible Chicken, it sounded as if it were a part of the raging elements. The uninhabited stage had a mood of plaintive lonelines and foreboding of catastrophe.

Thus before an actor had set foot on the stage, an alert theatre-goer might have recognized that the complicated and uneven history of Tennessee Williams on the Soviet stage had not been in vain. There had been an evident development toward understanding the playwright's theatrical language, his "plastic theatre" that he hoped would replace "the exhausted theatre of realistic conventions."[69]

The stage set in the Moscow Mossoviet Theatre, conceived by artist Mark Kitaev, looked quite similar to the Leningrad set. There was a longitudinal section of an old farmhouse. The elegant but neglected parlor and Chicken's dwelling-kitchen were on the first floor, and a bedroom was on the second. This room was illuminated by a bluish light and filled with laces, Miss Lottie's dresses, and family pictures, all the things that served to remind us of the faded, almost unreal beauty of the past--a ridiculous anachronism in this house threatened by flood. However, as so often had happened before with Soviet productions, Williams's symbolism was turned from the "purest language of plays,"[70] to use his own terms, into a literal illustration. The abundance of detail and the deadly bluish light accompanying Lot looked irritatingly illustrative. (As did the blood-red light illuminating the stage in the TTSA Orpheus, when Beulah was telling the story of Papa Romano; or the intense blue that flooded the stage with the arrival of the Gentleman Caller in the Perm Menagerie). Williams's language is figurative and poetic. His remarks are of great value for the theatre; however, simple allegiance to them never helped a director to succeed. His word should not be taken literally but considered as an adjunct to the play's structure of imagery.

Originally, Williams named the play The Seven Descents of Myrtle. Perhaps, with all the changes, it is a play for Myrtle--a play for the "warm-natured woman. You might say passionate even." Her pills from the Memphis doctor fail to restrain her natural calling to offer herself to all who express a need for her. That is why the approach to this character determines the interpretation of the play itself.

In the Mossoviet Theatre, Myrtle was played by Valentina Talyzina. Only in jest might this Myrtle have been called "The Petite Personality Kid." Her fussy curls and vulgar dresses spoke for her provincialism. As an imperious and irresistible proprietress she was pitiful. Behind the facade was visible the vulnerability of a woman who was not very young and not very clever. Her hope of finding a home and a family disappeared before our eyes. In the interpretation of Khomsky and Talyzina, Myrtle was a complete victim of the brothers' discord, an absolutely passive woman driven by events and subordinated to their inexorable logic. Her pity for Lot and her feeble desire to hang on to dignity and self-respect were swept away by fear of death and the urge to survive at any price. At Chicken's first request, she gave herself up to him; a submissive victim, she cared only for the promise of rescue. The director eliminated the motif of Myrtle's sexual desire for Chicken, thus narrowing her role.

In Williams's conception, however, Myrtle's instinct for survival is linked to her "warm" and "passionate" nature. In each of the seven scenes, she descends from the bedroom of the dying Lot to the kitchen, Chicken's abode. These successive encounters made possible the final ascent to the roof and rescue into the vision of a new life. According to Talyzina's interpretation, however, Lot was not of primary importance for Myrtle, although she pitied him. More important was her desire to be a wife and owner of a farm. Her Myrtle did not have "the deepest chord" in her nature; thus a very important aspect of the drama was lost. In Williams's conception, Myrtle nurses Lot absolutely unselfishly, even after she realizes that he has married her only to keep the family property from passing to his half-brother. She is dismayed only by the realization that he is indeed dying. (In the 1968 version, she has had five children but has lost them through adoption). The instinctual Chicken at once senses that she is the mother to all men, a woman searching for a place to hang her loving heart. Williams's Myrtle must give life and thus she receives it in return.

However, in the Moscow production, not much changed after the intimacy of Chicken and Myrtle, except that uncertainty and fear gave way to contentment. Lot died, but Talyzina-Myrtle was unmoved. A powerful boom announced the approaching flood waters. Looking victoriously out at his land, Chicken rushed to the roof with Myrtle. The company treated the play's text carefully and followed the author's remarks almost literally. However, it did not intend to reveal the drama's profound ideas. Where Williams suggests a complex system of conflicting motivations, the Mossoviet Theatre offered mere explanations that appeared simple and narrow-minded.

In Leningrad, Myrtle was played by Tatiana Tkach, and she became one of the striking successes of the production. The complex image of Williams's heroine was the joint creation of Tkach and the director, Kama Ginkas. This Myrtle, a former variety "diva" had two dreams--one of a Hollywood "paradise"; another of a quiet, secure family life. But as Lot's wife, this woman followed her beloved husband into a Sodom that was about to perish.

Williams mentions in <u>Kingdom of Earth</u> that the land to be destroyed by the symbolic Flood is Two River County, the hell he had described earlier in his <u>Orpheus Descending</u>. Ginkas thought of Myrtle as another variation of a Williams's Orpheus-like savior. He interpreted Williams's way of thinking as mythological. He wanted Tatiana Tkach to combine in her role concrete reality with "the general, the human, in other words with a myth," the essence of which was, in the words of Thomas Mann, "recurrence, timelessness, and everlasting presence."[71]

In the previous chapters, we discussed the fact that the Soviet theatre, with its strong realistic traditions, had difficulty in comprehending the mythological mode of Williams's <u>Glass Menagerie</u> or <u>Orpheus Descending</u>, with his use of timeless patterns and rituals. In 1982, in the Leningrad MDT, as we have seen, Geta Yanovska staged <u>The Glass Menagerie</u> as an endless ritual of loss and despair. But four years before that, her husband, Kama Ginkas, interpreted <u>Kingdom of Earth</u> as combining Biblical allusions with what he considered the favorite Williams's myth--that of the Orpheus-like artist.

The Leningrad Myrtle appeared on stage wearing extravagant checked pants. Her gait and way of speaking were those of someone trying in vain to do an imitation of a Hollywood glamour girl. From the beginning, however, this Myrtle made us aware of a soul filled with love and kindness. We could share her gentle discontent when she entered "her" house from the back door; we could understand her feelings when she was not allowed to sit in the gilded parlor chairs. Tkach was never unauthentic. She never played out of tune-- neither as the ridiculous, good-natured variety actress in search of a "quiet family life" nor as Lot's tormented wife enduring shock and revelation on the night of the flood. Of the three actors in this production, Tkach was the closest to understanding and portraying both the real and the mythological aspects of her character. When, at the beginning of the play, she rushed to Lot, exclaiming "Lot, dear, I'm not just your wife, I'm also your mother, and I'm not dead, I'm livin... " we became aware of the Orphic abilities of this woman. Her mission was to love, to restore, to liberate, to give re-birth. What kind of response did she get? "Don't sit on Mother's gold chairs."

"Do you know what life is based on?" asked Chicken. "Evil. I think it's evil," said Myrtle. For her, this conviction was a genuine one. Again the actress made us feel that she portrayed not just a sentimental whore but a complex woman with a mythological depth to her character. Here was a person who had descended into hell not merely for property or for "quiet family life" but because she was Lot's wife, and she believed Lot needed her. In the Leningrad production, Myrtle told about her five children lost to adoption because she could not support them. "My heart was broken five times," she confessed. "The deepest chord in my nature is the maternal chord in me."72 Lot's wife, driven by unfulfilled yearning to bestow maternal love, found another soul in hell where she arrived--coarse, embittered, and unfortunate Chicken. Myrtle-Tkach gave herself to Chicken only partly in fear for her life. She recognized that Lot, who was absorbed in his disease and preoccupied by his mother-complex, just used her. Genuinely desiring Chicken, she hoped to find with him re-birth through love and maternal compassion.

Ginkas connected love and freedom in a very definite sense. A human being's capacity for love, he believed, might be a great liberating force. Williams said: "What is opposite to death?" "Love, desire." Ginkas agreed with him. Probably this conviction was natural for an artist increasingly aware of the sense of futility, the dangerous passivity caused by official ideological propaganda. Courageously this director staged his production as a confirmatiom of a belief important both to Williams and to himself: the secret of healing our deepest wounds, the mystery of salvation from cruelty and living death lie, not in ideology or social reforms, but in love and compassion. He wanted to show that humanity, wallowing in vice and threatened by flood, could be saved by the strength of Myrtle's ability to love.

Perplexed and terrified, Myrtle-Tkach denied her marriage to Lot and wrote the "letter" Chicken demanded. However, she fulfilled her Orphic calling and led Chicken to the culminating scene. Obeying Williams's direction, she looked as if "she had undergone an experience of exceptional nature and magnitude."73 In this scene Chicken defined the "Kingdom of Earth:"

> Nothing in the world ... can compare with one thing, and that one thing is what's able to happen between a man and a woman, just this thing, nothing more, is perfect. The rest is crap ... If you never had nothing else but that, no property, no success in the world ... why, I say, this life would be worth something ... That's how I look at it, that's how I see it now, in this Kingdom of Earth.74

Ginkas was not afraid of stressing that sexual love could transform human existence from something barren into something rich and glorious. We remember, how in the Mayakovsky Streetcar, Blanche was portrayed without her morbid sexuality and turned into a kind of sexless, romantic heroine. We have discussed the bigoted misrepresentation of the meaning of sexual relationships in Orpheus and Sweet Bird. Ginkas' Kingdom was among the first Soviet productions marked by an open, honest attitude toward sex.

Ginkas and Tkach never tried to veil the sexual attraction between Myrtle and Chicken. They brought Williams's famous "magic touch" to the letter-writing scene when Chicken held Myrtle's hand. In her seven descents Myrtle also revealed a changing definition of love. In this production, as Williams intended, Myrtle moved from her pure sacrificial motherliness to the resumption of her real sexual self.

In analyzing the Leningrad production, it is important to mention Myrtle's costumes, created by designer Irene Gabay. Instead of a long skirt made from "washable velvet"75 and a spangled blouse, this "Petite Personality Kid" appeared in a frivolous red dress--a tasteless "cafe chantant diva" whose image had been worn out by the screen and cheap novels. In another scene she wore an undisguised bikini with little wings on her back--a naive and pitiable fallen angel. The director and the company not only tried to stress the commonplace quality of Williams's heroine (as was done in Moscow) but also to point out the romance in her role and the fate to which she was predestined. Kama Ginkas had Myrtle sing "Heavenly

Grass," the ballad sung by Val Xavier in <u>Orpheus Descending</u> (According to the text, Myrtle sings "It is what they say about Dixie"). Despite Myrtle's bikini and vulgar behavior, the director wanted to suggest her Orphic quality, her ability to bring people together with a song. "Do you have a guitar?" Myrtle asked rapturously. Temporarily forgetting her fears of Chicken and of the flood, she sang the song of Williams's Orpheus. This indicated the producer's almost sentimental dream of forgotten values--purity, beauty, sincerity.

Tkach showed us how Myrtle craved, perhaps unconsciously, a revival of kindness and humanity. Wanting to bring some meaning to life in a basically evil world, Myrtle put her faith in art. After her illusion of a "quiet family life" had been broken, she exclaimed: "Now what I want most in the world is to return to show business! ... It keeps you alive ... Absolutely no other can compare with it for keeping you healthy and active."76

As we have seen, the most explicit among Williams's Orpheuses, Val Xavier, in the TTSA production, had nothing to do with his ancient artist-protagonist. We discussed in the previous chapter, how the whole meaning of Williams's conception of the Orphic myth was subverted. However, theatrical development occurs in ways that are not always logical or straightforward. It happened that Williams's ideas of art and artist began to be comprehended and expressed not in the production of <u>Orpheus</u>, but in the Leningrad version of the "strange" and "funny" play, <u>Kingdom of Earth</u>. For Kama Ginkas and Tatiana Tkach, art was the symbol of a soul's ability to rise above the general lack of spirituality. That was why a vulgar, variety "diva" was given the Orphic function. Myrtle-Tkach, terrified but compassionate, rushed between kitchen and bedroom seeking to help two people who had touched "the deepest chord" in her nature. Finally she was able to fling open the "spiritual gate" of one of them.

Tkach played the finale simply and strictly. She did not rush upstairs but stayed motionless, facing the audience. She gave no heed to Chicken's comand: "Myrtle, give me your hand!" She seemed to see nothing around her but rather to be listening attentively to something inside herself: "The deepest chord in my nature--Don't that river sound louder? Or am I just more scared to death of it?"77 The audience was charmed by the actress' modest and truthful muse. "The Petite Personality Kid" in this production turned into an eminent person in Williams's hell.

In both productions, the atmosphere of cold animosity and mutual cruelty between the brothers was interpreted as natural for a world wallowing in vice. However, the two approaches to the brothers' characters were absolutely different. In the Mossoviet Theatre, Lot was played by a very popular actor, Gennady Bortnikov. From the very beginning he was spiritually dead and his Lot remained static throughout the performance. All his movements and intonations were full of affectation and self-admiration. Bortnikov thoroughly selected and exaggerated the poses and gestures of his character. The actor's usual acting manner--"these inconceivable eyes, these hands reaching out ... " (as he was described by one of his admirers)--was spectacular and old-fashioned. In this performance, it looked like a deliberate coquetry with the audience. Bortnikov concentrated his attention excessively on the pathology of his character. This Lot belonged to the world upstairs--Miss Lottie's bedroom. Fetishes from the past dictated his desire to keep his half-brother from inheriting the farm. Bortnikov emphasized these fetishes along with Lot's sufferings; they provided the only meaning of his character's existence. According to the script, Lot tried to overcome and conceal his weakness especially in front of Chicken; Bortnikov, however, from his first moments on the stage, concentrated on his disease and displayed it forcefully.

The dramatical pivot of Lot's part should be his gradual self-disclosure. However, Bortnikov revealed himself to the audience immediately, thus provoking censure without understanding. This approach was rejected by the famous drama critic Komissarzhevsky, who asked in his review:

> Why is Lot dying? ... Because of tuberculosis or because of the metastases of his greed and racial hatred? Lot does not have to demonstrate his physical sickness but to overcome it. Only then will his diseased attitude be revealed; the refined prince turns into an ordinary racist. The role, that is static now,

has to be put in motion.78

In Leningrad, Kama Ginkas, as a director, and V. Belovolsky, as an actor, suggested their own interpretation of this role. It was different from both Bortnikov's coquetry and from Komissarzhevsky's concept of Lot's gradual disclosure of his social and racial interior. At first, Belovolsky's character seemed very close to that of Bortnikov: the same contrast of outer refinement and inner futility. Belovolsky emphasized the effeminacy and delicacy of Lot; he was beautiful but callous.

This Lot, like Bortnikov's, accepted Myrtle's love condescendingly, seeming indifferent to everything except his own disease and Miss Lottie's legacy of elegance. In both productions Lot spent almost all his time upstairs, literally living "above" life. In both productions there was the traditional Williams conflict between sensibility and sensuality, between beauty and brute force. In both, refinement and aristocracy co-existed with futility, disease, arrogance and lack of spirituality. Pavel Khomsky, the Moscow director, probably had a similar conception to that of Ginkas. However, it did not come out clearly in Bortnikov's performance because the actor used the role for his own purposes, while in Leningrad something was introduced that the Moscow performance lacked--irony.

Ginkas was interested in exploring in a profound way the hallucinatory quality of human existence offered by the play. He conceived of the drama in terms of two opposing "kingdoms." While in Moscow it was not always clear what the title had to do with the action, in Leningrad the connection was clearly defined. There was the Kingdom of Earth, which Chicken advocated, and there was the Kingdom of Heaven, which an evangelist had once told him to seek by restraining his "lustful body."79 Lot re-enforced the contrast with his ironic asceticism. He told Myrtle: "You've married someone to whom no kind of sex relations was ever as important as fighting sickness and trying with his mother to make, to create, a little elegance in a corner of the earth we lived in that was not favorable to it."80

Gradually Belovolsky made us understand: Lot's perception of life--this sexless Kingdom of Heaven--was nothing but an amusing jest. This Lot did not really pursue his own objective; he was false to his Kingdom as he defined it. In the gilded world of elegance and grace there was a chain of lies. Lot took after his mother and he was as false as she had been. The elegant parlor, the taste and style, were only a facade to mask her pursuit of the Kingdom of Earth. Miss Lottie, as we know from Chicken, was not a spiritual aristocrat but a greedy sensualist. She had "begun to cheat on" her husband soon after her marriage with "a good-looking Greek fellow that had a fruit store in town."[81] The falsity of Lot's spiritual pretensions was revealed when Belovolsky ironically confessed to having bleached blond hair. His veneration for beauty, advocated by Miss Lottie, his mother, was really the result of the dark instinct that possessed his soul, the Oedipus complex that burdened his consciousness. His grace and elegance were merely an ironic facade to conceal his meaninglessness, and Belovolsky as Lot was the first to portray it.

Amidst Lot's complex emotions regarding Chicken, there was more than just hatred, more than a desire for vengeance against one who was stronger. There was also a kind of ambiguity. Chicken was always present in Lot's mind and Belovolsky illustrated it, usually by means of a toy, a little yellow chicken that he carried in his pocket and played with often. Neither he nor Ginkas were afraid of thinking in terms of the Freudian categories that were usually hushed up in Soviet theatre as if they never existed. In weak and feminine Lot there was something of a perverted love for the strong and masculine Chicken and Belovolsky conveyed it.

Ginkas saw in Lot one of the "wispy, willowy women" Williams had written about, even though he was unfamiliar with Mike Stein's anthology of Williams's interviews and therefore with Williams's comment to Estelle Parsons (cited above). For the first time on the Soviet stage, Williams had begun to speak of something important that tormented him: homosexual feelings. Ginkas' attempt to look openly at this aspect of Williams's work has never been continued. When <u>Cat on a Hot Tin Roof</u> was staged in Moscow and Leningrad (1982 and 1983), Brick's only problem was his good nature and unwillingness to cope with a false world.

Lot's Kingdom of Heaven represented both his hidden desire for Chicken's earthly "kingdom" and his relationship with his mother whom he attempted to "resurrect" by transvestic donning of her clothing. For Ginkas, this sterile kingdom full of falsehood could only be the Kingdom of Death. Lot-Belovolsky, as transvestite, looking "bizarre and beautiful" (as Williams described it), gave his performance the quality of a transfiguration when he descended to death amidst the gold and crystal of Miss Lottie, but close to the earthly dwelling of Chicken.

Belovolsky created a complex image. His ironic character understood the futility of his pretensions. Although heartless and often repulsive, he was a figure for whom the audience could not help but feel compassion. On the Moscow stage, Bortnikov, too, played a suffering Lot, but he was not able to attract such compassion. Indeed the importance of the element of compassion was not adequately understood in the one-dimensional Moscow production. (Likewise, in the MXAT Sweet Bird, the company did not consider it necessary for Chance to appeal to the audience for compassion.) However, Kama Ginkas felt that compassion was not merely an ethical consideration but actually an aesthetic component for Williams--one that expanded the boundaries of his plays. Compassion could enrich a character by means of unexpected and contradictory nuances, thereby giving rise to understanding and perhaps even wisdom. Compassion could make opportunites for kindness and humanity where they might have seemed totally absent. In Ginkas' production, for example, Chicken himself conveyed Lot's lifeless body to the sofa almost tenderly. However, compassion and tenderness, like emotional ambiguity, were not considered suitable for Chicken in the Moscow production.

Here he was played by a famous actor, Georgy Zhzhenov. Having earned his popularity in the movies, Zhzhenov remained "cinematographic" on the stage, mechanically transferring his screen methods to the theatre. But theatre and cinema work through different "quantums of energy," different temperaments and tensions of the inner world. What is true for the theatre often appears as untrue for the screen and vice versa.

Williams's Chicken, a mulatto and an outsider, could be hideous, bawdy and unbearable, but then, in a burst of pain and anguish, he was able to reveal what had been tormenting him for years. Zhzhenov was very "cinematographic" and discreet in his performance, but he had nothing to restrain. His Chicken lacked the shackled inner rage that could suddenly break loose. His intimacy with Myrtle meant nothing important. It was neither a revelation of his own full value nor the discovery that love and tenderness remained in this world. His philosophy concerning his "spiritual gate" seemed improper and tactless against the background of death. Like the meaning of the play, the image of Chicken was simplified in the Moscow theatre. Although Zhzhenov did speak reverently of sex, what he really appeared to pursue was only the ownership of the farm. For one who would give up food and water to sleep in a shack with a middle-aged woman, this Chicken was too single-mindedly materialistic. Both characters and ideas in this production were truncated in a way that diminished the compassion and emotional involvement of the spectators.

On the Leningrad stage, on the other hand, Chicken was returned to his polyphonic meaning. He was played by Ermolaev. In this actor's repertoire there were many roles from Western European and American drama, such as McMurphy in Ken Kesey's One Flew Over the Cuckoo's Nest and Stanley in Streetcar. He had done main parts in Edward Albee's plays. As an actor, Ermolaev was able to sense and convey the inadequacies of Williams's characters. As Chicken, the dark-complexioned Ermolaev was strange and somehow attractive. He was full of strength and masculine grace. He was also one of the "brutes," as his name suggested; that name apparently derived from his brutal practice of catching chickens, biting their heads off and drinking their blood when he was waiting out the floods while perched on the roof. But the actor convinced us that, although he could be rough, obscene, scandalous, there was a tender side to this charater-- also represented by his name in its slang meaning of cowardice. Unlike the Moscow Chicken with his indifference to women, Ermolaev conveyed an almost touching fear of them. This, of course, he had tried to conceal by hanging a picture of a nude girl in the kitchen. But when Lot arrived with Myrtle, Chicken crouched behind the door, remaining in the kitchen until he had fortified himself for the encounter by means of whisky.

It was very important for Kama Ginkas and Ermolaev, that their Chicken lack hatred completely; there had to be corners in his soul open to kindness and humanity, even to love. Ermolaev succeeded in expressing the complex gamut of feelings. His Chicken despised the subtle Lot and his refined ideals; he tried to humiliate and hurt him. But at the same time, he rubbed Lot's temples tenderly when his half-brother was about to faint in the kitchen scene, and, as mentioned above, he showed the same tenderness in carrying Lot's lifeless body to the parlor. Unrestricted by bigotry, the director of this production was not afraid to show the complexity of feelings between these two charaters.

Ermolaev played Chicken's brutality as the mask he had to wear as the unwanted. Beneath his seeming indifference was a passion for generativeness; for completion of some potential in himself by means of another (either Lot or a woman), for extension of that self through identification with what he called the "Kingdom of Earth." Perhaps most of all there was a need for tenderness and compassion.

The actor saw Chicken as one denied not only attention and cordiality but even the cheap love of a prostitute. Chicken's bitter disposition was easily accounted for by such morbid suppressions in the social and psychosexual spheres. Ermolaev made Chicken's primeval animality obvious. He was a survivor— single-minded and brutal: he survived any floods, and he brutally mishandled Myrtle. He lived in the disordered kitchen amidst the food and heat (passion), amusing himself by carving obscenities on the table.

We have to emphasize, however, that the actor had a very important sense of limits. Ermolaev never portrayed vulgarity and roughness by vulgar and rough means. And he did not excuse the mercenary aspirations of his character. After all, each of the three sought self-possession in the Ravenstock property. It meant both a sign of acceptance and a sense of home. Of course it was Myrtle who spoke for them all, at their best, when she assured Lot that not all desperate people thought only of themselves.

Immediately after their intimacy, Chicken said, "Let there be light," and then inquired whether Myrtle had ever been saved. "Yes," she answered. "I've been saved by you." But to the director's mind it was Chicken who was saved by Myrtle from being buried alive in the hell of hostility and brutality. Ermolaev acted an explosion—a sudden outburst of thoughts and feelings that had been locked up inside Chicken's being for years. His confession to Myrtle was a statement of self-recognition. Ginkas stressed the grandeur of what was happening between Myrtle and Chicken by a solemn chorale. It was clear that Chicken was thinking physically not spiritually, but the stage-director gave him the gift of premonition of the coming salvation. "God is spirit," Ermolaev read in the beginning of the second act. "All-good and ubiquitous."

Ermolaev's character lived by a stark philosophy based upon personal satisfaction:

> With human beings, the ones I known in my life, what counts is personal satisfaction, and God knows you'll never get that by denying yourself what you want most in the world by straining and struggling for what they call salvation when it is something you're just not cut out for.[82]

Williams's God, like Ginkas', probably did know that salvation and personal satisfaction were not antithetical but inseparable. In the Leningrad production, this was the meaning of the "Kingdom of Earth."

Ermolaev succeeded in suggesting Chicken's almost primeval propinquity to nature. His first appearance on the stage—a big man in rubber boots, a suitable antagonist to a flooding river—indicated that he was clearly a life force. Water was emphasized in this performance as a symbol of Chicken's association with elemental nature. We were not allowed to forget that beneath Lot's "kingdom," the upstairs bedroom and the elegant parlor, there was a cellar swirling with water. Symbolically, the depth of the water was unknown, but its roar was heard constantly. On the Moscow stage it was difficult to connect the raging river with Zhzhenov's performance as Chicken. But for Ermolaev, fear was absolutely inconceivable. His character was as elemental as the flood. "Life, rock. Man, rock,"[83] he said.

In the Liteiny Theatre, the flood was treated as the reminder of the Old Testament. The world, weak, mendacious, corrupt, was before its executioner. Everything had to be cleared away, including elegance and beauty. But after the raging and purifying Flood, despite all the dirt of human life, Myrtle would probably bear Chicken's child and begin to populate the

"Kingdom of Earth." As Lot's wife, she had not been turned into a pillar of salt when she "looked back," leaving the "Kingdom of Heaven" which Lot represented. Williams wanted her to survive and become a living inhabitant of the "Kingdom of Earth." When Chicken threw the cat into the cellar it also survived.

The message of Ginkas' production was clear. It was survival. Probably he had his own fears close to those of Williams: were we going into an era of Stanleys and Chickens? It was the common man, the grossman (Mr. Grossman) Williams calls him in the <u>Two Character Play</u>, who prosper. Was it the strong, brutal, and rising lower class who would inherit the earth? This kind of terror has long been very familiar to Russian intelligentsia. Far back, in his <u>Demons</u>, Dostoevsky wrote of the coming kingdom of a cad who would spit upon ideals and beauty. However, Ginkas' production was neither tragic nor pessimistic. It carried no "hostile" ideas either. It was simply the serious and honest attempt of a talented artist to define love, compassion, and understanding between people--in any conditions, before any catastrophe--as the only means for salvation and survival. The audience, those who love and understand Williams, turned out in force every night <u>Kingdom of Earth</u> was given.

NOTES

60 Tennessee Williams, Memoirs (New York: Nelson Doubleday, Inc., 1975), p. 40.

61 Tennessee Williams, Kingdom of Earth in The Theatre of Tennessee Williams (New York: New Directions, 1976), V, 211.

62 Quot. in Mike Stein, A Look at Tennessee Williams (New York: Hawthorn, 1969), p. 272.

63 Quot. in Stein, p. 265.

64 Quot. in Stein, p. 266.

65 Signi Falk, Tennessee Williams (Boston: Twayne Publishers, 1978), pp. 129, 134.

66 Tennessee Williams, Orpheus Descending, p. 575.

67 V. Vulf, "Tennessi Uilyams i Ego Pesa," v Teatralnoy Programme k spektaklyu Tsarstvie Zemnoe. Moskovky Teatr imeni Mossoveta, 1977. (V. Vulf, "Tennessee Williams and His Play," in the Theatre Program for the production of Kingdom of Earth. Moscow Mossoviet Theatre, 1977).

68 Tennessee Williams, "Production Notes" to The Glass Menagerie, p. 9.

69 Tennessee Williams, "Production Notes" to The Glass Menagerie, p. 10.

70 Tennessee Williams, "Foreword" to Camino Real (New York: New Directions, 1958), p. xi.

71 Quot. in Joseph Strelka, Literary Criticism and Myth (Philadelphia: University Press, 1980), p. 27.

72 Tennessee Williams, Kingdom of Earth, p. 135.

73 Tennessee Williams, Kingdom of Earth, p. 203.

74 Tennessee Williams, Kingdom of Earth, p. 211.

75 Tennessee Williams, Kingdom of Earth, p. 157.

76 Tennessee Williams, Kingdom of Earth, p. 189.

77 Tennessee Williams, *Kingdom of Earth*, p. 214.

78 V. Komissarzhevsky, "Lestnitsa na Kryshu: Pesy Tennissi Uilyamsa na Sovetskoy Stsene," *Sovetskaya Kultura*, 28 Fevr. 1978. (V. Komissarzhevsky, "Stairs to the Roof: Tennessee Williams's Plays on the Soviet Stage," *Soviet Culture*, 28 Febr. 1978).

79 Tennessee Williams, *Kingdom of Earth*, p. 210.

80 Tennessee Williams, *Kingdom of Earth*, p. 160.

81 Tennessee Williams, *Kingdom of Earth*, p. 187.

82 Tennessee Williams, *Kingdom of Earth*, p. 210.

83 Tennessee Williams, *Kingdom of Earth*, p. 192.

EPILOGUE

We see that a foreign drama, when staged, inevitably becomes an integral part of that culture and that language in which it is played. A book of translated prose or poetry may be forgotten and collect dust somewhere on the shelf. The theatre is different. Through translated drama, the people of the theatre--consciously or not--introduce their own thoughts, associations, and their own ideas of life and art. Williams's "funny melodrama," a strange medley of the Biblical Flood and "Rabelaisian characters", that was a failure in its own country, happened to be the play closest to Russian self-consciousness and its production was a significant step in the process of comprehending Western drama by the Soviet theatre.

Very often, especially in a country like the Soviet Union, such an event can occur with no official acknowledgment. There were no reviews about the Leningrad production of <u>Kingdom</u>. Not a word was said in the press about one of the most interesting Soviet "Williamses."

Looking at the various Soviet productions of Tennessee Williams, we see that artistic development is not a linear process. It is a continuing alternation of gears and brakes, and very often it seems that the brakes are always in action. However, there is hope for better understanding between different cultures and for artistic progress. This hope is given to us by the ever-living wonder--the Theatre. "Our serious theatre is a search for that something that is not yet successful but is still going on,"[84] Williams believed.

NOTES

[84] Tennessee Williams, "Foreword" to *Sweet Bird of Youth*, p. 645.